PRAYING TOGETHER

Praying Together

Mike & Katey Morris

KINGSWAY PUBLICATIONS
EASTBOURNE

ISBN 0 86065 496 6

Produced by Bookprint Creative Services
P.O. Box 827, BN21 3YJ, England for
KINGSWAY PUBLICATIONS LTD
Lottbridge Drove, Eastbourne, E. Sussex, BN23 6NT.
Printed in Great Britain

To our parents
who suffer so much of the criticism
and receive so little
of the credit.
Thanks.

Contents

Foreword

People who write books on prayer are often thought to be predictable, set in their ways and 'well stricken in years'. However, there is nothing stuffy or formal about Mike and Katey Morris. Their obvious joy in the Lord—and in each other—bubbles over, making a deep and lasting impression on the reader. Behind Mike's puckish appearance is a very fine mind (honoured by Oxford University) and a spiritual maturity which those who know him best deeply respect and honour. Katey's ebullience could easily mask a gentle caring heart and an ability to cope with disappointment and turn it into creative testimony.

In this book they show how prayer touches three worlds at the same time. It touches heaven since prayer affects God more than anything else. It touches earth since prayer affects man at a depth and a reality beyond anything else. And it touches hell since prayer disturbs the devil more than any other human enterprise. The whole emphasis of Mike and Katey's writing is on the limitless power of prayer and how this can be experienced in practical ways in our day-to-day living.

They would not underestimate the value of praying alone. Indeed, they show we are never really alone when we pray, for God the Father is listening, God the Son is involved and God the Holy Spirit draws alongside to help. The angels also come into the picture, as do the demons of darkness. But the aim of this book is to highlight the joy and effectiveness of praying together. This they do with great honesty.

I am privileged to commend this book to you. I know the authors, and love and trust them. I also know the realities of which they speak and believe the truth of what they write.

JIM GRAHAM

Introduction

'Surely not another book on prayer! And what's more, praying with one's partner! This is too much. I've been told to pray ever since I stumbled into the kingdom of God, and I still haven't got it together. What's more, if I pray with my partner it's even worse—so we don't. I can certainly do without a lecture on what I ought to be doing.'

If this is your immediate reaction hold on just one more minute before you throw this book down in frustration. This book is not really a book—it's a manual. Quite simply, a practical guide to help us all to learn how to pray together. We promise you at the outset it is not a lecture nor the confessions of a mystic's successful encounters with God to make you feel more miserable.

Throughout the book you will find that some of the headings appear in **bold italic** type, with a symbol (▶). This means that there is something to pause and think about, commit to memory, or put into immediate action by 'having a go'.

Suddenly you feel a wave of panic sweeping through you. A book that actually demands action? Well, yes. As we've said, we have designed it as a manual, with a very practical approach to prayer, providing everything you need to lay the foundations for an effective prayer life together. As with any manual, it will teach you and enable you to become proficient at putting the contents into practice.

The book actually took shape following a series of seminars entitled 'How to pray with your partner', which we ran at Spring Harvest in 1984. These seminars took the form of practical workshops, and we were amazed at the number of people who crowded in. In the months and years following we have had letters from and met a good number of couples who came to those seminars with a poverty of prayer experience together, and yet from that point on have discovered an effective and, I'm glad to say, enjoyable prayer life together.

We believe that if worked through, this book will produce some fruit in your life together. It is intended, in current jargon, for 'hands on' experience—not simply being talked at, but responding by doing. Each chapter is self-contained and can be read on its own. Ideally you read the book in tandem—i.e. you both read together—and hence two copies would not go amiss. When we say, 'Get together with your partner,' that's what we mean. Don't go through the 'Action Stations' on your own—that rather defeats the object of the book.

The book is intended for couples at whatever stage they are, whether married, engaged or just going out together. We know you will have a lot of fun putting the content into practice. So go for it and let us know how you get on.

I

Prayer Is a Problem

What a negative title for a chapter! However, read on because I believe that phrase is the one on more Christians' lips than any other. From the moment we make our entrance into God's kingdom as 'soundly saved' individuals, we are assaulted from every quarter with exhortations to pray. Very quickly we take on board the assumption that every real Christian prays and our salvation is in doubt if we find we don't, so to admit to such a failure becomes an impossibility—we would probably be stoned or some twentieth-century equivalent!

In a recent survey individuals were asked how much time they spent praying in a day. Honesty was demanded and to some degree guaranteed through anonymity. The results were hailed as shocking and surprising: Mr & Mrs Average prayed approximately five minutes every day. And yet does that figure really shock you? When I heard the results I found them an affront to my Christian 'outer garment', but that which lurked within, i.e. the real me, was not at all surprised because the results reflected my experience.

Just to check it through further, the same questionnaire was circulated to a random number of clergy. The result was exactly the same, which if it proves nothing else demonstrates a dog-collar does not remove one's humanity!

Now the purpose of this book, as stated, is praying together. So why not, right now, pause and jot down how long you as an individual spend in prayer on average every day. And then how long you spend in prayer on average as a couple together.

Before you feel utterly condemned (years of exhortation about prayer leaves us brimful with condemnation because we haven't ever got it sorted), just remember you are no different from Mr & Mrs Average as revealed in the survey, and maybe better. What's more, you are as competent as your spiritual leader so that should encourage you.

At the Spring Harvest seminars, when Katey and I asked, 'How many of you have a regular and effective prayer life together?' only half a dozen hands out of about 400 would go up. We all start in the same boat. You are not alone but share the same experience as countless thousands of people. The good news is that prayer does not have to remain a problem, and if you work through this manual consistently we can assure you that your prayer life stands every chance of being dramatically improved.

Getting to grips with the task

Imagine a Sunday morning—one of those long slow wake-up days when nothing is going to be demanded of you. As consciousness dawns you remember it's Sunday, a day off, so you luxuriate with a stretch and drift back into unconsciousness. This process can continue for a long time if, like ours, your church has no morning service.

It was one such Sunday when, with great gallantry, I had tumbled out of bed and made my way downstairs to make the tea and pick up the paper. (Ours being a house of distinction we take the *Sunday Times;* the one problem is that having paid out for it, the whole day can be marred by the pressure to read it all to get one's money's worth.) I returned, tray in hand, and climbed back into bed where Katey and I began to survey the paper. As usual I ploughed into the news and Katey wandered through the supplement.

All was well until Katey interrupted my attempts to grasp the Middle Eastern situation with a sharp nudge indicating that I look at the magazine. My eyes took in the title 'The ABC Diet Plan' and my heart sank. 'Just what we need!' exclaimed Katey. It was at that moment in time I considered revoking my TV licence because just two weeks before, as the screen projected scores of eager runners jogging round the streets of London, I had made the rash statement that I fancied getting fit and having a go. Now, as if to mock my athletic ambition, the *Sunday Times* in all its wisdom was providing a step-by-step approach to fitness. Katey, with her normal rash enthusiasm, declared this was for us. We would follow the schedule week by week and within a year compete in the London Marathon.

Well, the weeks passed. We collected, read, appreciated and filed the supplements, and yet neither of us improved in stamina, strength or suppleness. The problem, as you may have guessed, was that although we had clear intentions to get fit and lose some fat, and even though we had a well produced, step-by-step guide for achieving it, we never actually put it into practice. And there's the rub! Belief is only valuable when it is accompanied by the will to act. God has always recognized that 'faith without works is dead'. We did not have the will to turn our good intentions to practical effect.

Some years later we are not measurably fitter. Similarly with our prayer life, we can have all the Scripture, all the teaching, all the tapes, videos and books we like— but if we won't decide to *do* something positive our prayer life will continue at the low level we currently experience. However, if we will agree to do something positive—like read this book and work through the exercises—our prayer life can and will improve. Ask each other now what you are going to do about it. Are you prepared to get 'stuck in' in concrete ways? Read on.

What does Jesus think?

The great news is that not only do we appreciate we have a problem, but Jesus knows we have one too. Interestingly enough, when Jesus was asked by the disciples about prayer he did not deliver a lecture but taught them the 'how to' of prayer. In fact it was the practical 'how to' that the disciples were keen to learn, as Luke 11:1-4 reveals.

I can imagine the disciples observing Jesus drawing aside to spend time discussing issues with his Father. There was a tremendous amount of pressure upon Jesus, and he always consulted his Father about what he should do; he never did anything that his Father did not want him to do. The disciples who travelled with Jesus also ate with him, slept by him and generally observed him at close hand. Thus they could see the benefit in Jesus' life of drawing aside and just taking time with the Father— and they wanted to get in on the action for themselves. Just imagine them observing Jesus praying, and asking one another, 'What's he doing?', 'Why don't we go and ask him?', and eventually summoning up the courage to go to him and put their request before him, 'Teach us how to pray like you pray.'

Yet having shared intimately with Jesus for three years, as well as having the 'how to' of prayer, the disciples still 'blew it' when Jesus asked them to pray in Gethsemane (Lk 22:39-46). They demonstrated that simply knowing is not sufficient in itself, but that we develop and learn as much, if not more, by the mistakes we make as well as the things we get right. Falling asleep did not mean the disciples couldn't care a fig about Jesus, they were simply exhausted and quite naturally fell asleep. Often the principle is not the problem, it's the practice.

Katey and I have been married for nearly nine years. Ours is a good marriage. I love Katey very much and cannot imagine life without her. I want to please her and ensure her happiness. However, in spite of these noble desires there are times, and not that infrequent, when we will have a conversation, usually while I am reading a book or watching the television, in which I promise to fetch something, purchase something or phone some-one. I then instantly forget these promises and fail to perform the task. Although this occasionally produces a fair measure of exasperation on Katey's part, it is not evidence of lack of love on my part—it is one of the realities of life and marriage.

So also with God. He fully appreciates the problems we humans have with prayer. He does not expect you to pledge yourself to a three hour vigil every night. He understands when having promised faithfully to pray for sick Aunt Mathilda you forget to do so until reminded by a phone call thanking you for your prayers. God created us human, he therefore fully appreciates the nature of our humanity. He is intimately interested in our praying, he is fully committed to guiding us in the 'how to' of prayer, and he totally appreciates the problems we have and the mistakes we make and the failures we experience. But, as you'd expect, he urges us to keep going and discover the development we can make. God is on our side rooting for us so let's get on with it.

Returning to the illustration of good old Aunt Mathilda, why not make it a practice that when someone asks you for your prayers that you pray for them right there and then. It's a practice that was suggested to us by Doug Barnett and one that we've made our own. If nothing else we have at least honoured our word in praying for the particular situation that the person has asked us to remember. It's a great practice to get into together. Often when I return home from being away on a ministry weekend or from the Evangelical Alliance the first thing we'll do when I come through the door, after a heart-warming kiss, is to hug one another and pray, thanking God for his goodness in keeping us and bringing us back together and for the good things that we've enjoyed.

Learning from personal experience

It was among the dreaming spires of Oxford while studying at the University that I became a Christian. While sitting in St Aldate's listening to the then Bishop of Coventry, the Rt Rev. Cuthbert Bardsley, describing the person of Jesus, I decided that if Jesus was all that he was claimed to be by the Bishop, I'd better go and find out more. I did, Jesus was and I was placed in a 'beginners' group' to learn the basis of being a Christian.

I remember early on in my Christian life that the need to read the Bible and pray was a daily imperative for every proper Christian. When you've got no Christian background you follow everything you're told to the letter, and so I would sit in my room and read my Bible and pray every day. I remember the first vacation from university following my conversion. Every day I read the Bible and prayed—I think my parents were a bit over-whelmed by this strange new behaviour—but it was so boring and apparently meaningless. Hard though I tried, it was about as exciting as a test-match interrupted by rain! However, being a great perseverer I steadfastly continued and was glad to get back to Oxford to ask some questions about this activity.

The questions were soon answered. Every sermon I heard about prayer was that God said one of two things: either he said, 'No,' in answer to our prayers or he said, 'Wait' (this was only so that he could say, 'No,' later!). It seemed that God called us to pray, only to turn down our many intercessions. Indeed, the fact of answered prayer was totally beyond my experience, apart from the very odd occasion, such as when I led Katey to Christ follow-ing half an hour of private intercession to that end, as much to build up my courage as to see God's kingdom extended.

It was at some point at this stage that, having faithfully read my Bible daily, I discovered that God was not one who only said, 'Wait,' or, 'No,' in response to our prayers. Indeed, he had a very positive attitude to prayer. Take, for example, the words of Jesus in Mark 11:24, 'When you pray and ask for something, believe that you have received it, and you will be given whatever you ask for.' That sounded pretty positive to me and a very clear statement from the lips of the Son of God. With the stipulation of verse 25 it became even clearer. I avidly looked up other references to prayer in the gos-pels. In Luke 11:9-10 Jesus says,

> Ask, and you will receive; seek, and you will find; knock, and the door will be opened to you. For everyone who asks will receive, and he who seeks will find, and the door will be opened to anyone who knocks.

Here Jesus clearly supported the view that God was in the business of answering prayer. The word 'everyone' in verse 10 meant this was true even for wallies like me. I lapped this up. This was good news indeed. In fact it was what I'd expected of God when I became a Christian, but had since lost sight of in seeking to take on board the 'Christian converts" package and conform to it as a new disciple wanting to do the decent and expected thing.

Words such as those in John 14:13—'And I will do whatever you ask for in my name, so that the Father's glory will be shown through the Son'—continued to develop a picture of a God who was committed to me and who expected me to be committed to him. My love was such that I wanted him to be pleased with me and I wanted extravagantly to give all that I knew of myself to all that I knew of him. I began to realize that the people, situations and personal needs that I had prayed about were all as important to God as they were to me and he wanted to get involved in a way that would highlight who he was and what he was about.

It was John 16:23-24 that finally clinched it for me—

> I am telling you the truth: the Father will give you whatever you ask for in my name. Until now you have not asked for anything in my name; ask and you will receive, so that your happiness may be complete.

I had not asked anything in Jesus' name in any other sense than fulfilling the Christian's responsibility to pray —not expecting God would acknowledge the request with an answer. Indeed, I was grateful that I had been taught that the Bible was a true and trustworthy manual for the life of the Christian disciple, because I could practically accept all the above promises and if that wasn't enough have them all underlined with 2 Corinthians 1:20, 'It is he who is the "Yes" to all God's promises. This is why through Jesus Christ our "Amen" is said to the glory of God.'

I emerged from this journey through the Scriptures enthused and informed, and it acted as a turning point in my Christian life and indeed ultimately in our prayer life together.

Word and experience

One of the consequences of growing up, apart from grey hair, is that one's perspective on life and indeed one's expectations from life are directly affected by one's experiences. In spite of a fine 'macho' image, Mike is petrified of going to the dentist. Indelibly imprinted on his mind are the memories of bleak days of childhood amidst the normally joyous school holidays. These were the six-monthly trips to the dentist. He can still recall the churning stomach and blind fear which gripped him on the morning of such trips as he ferociously brushed his teeth for twenty minutes hoping this would assure him of a clean bill of health. On the trip to the surgery everything else paled into insignificance as his mind concentrated upon the forthcoming encounter with the masked driller!

The waiting-room, comfortably set out and with a plethora of colourful magazines, was filled with equally nervous-looking people, all apparently reading or holding conversations in hushed tones but everyone with an ear to the whine of the dentist's drill. Once in the chair, somehow immortalized for Mike on TV through *Mastermind*, it was a case of gripping the arms of the chair till the knuckles turned white, opening one's mouth and locking it in an extremely uncomfortable position, screwing up the eyes as tightly as possible, and grunting incomprehensibly in response to the dentist's barked commands of, 'Relax!', 'Open wider!' and, 'I'm not going to hurt you,' which he promptly did!

Experiences like this at the hands of a man, who became affectionately known in the Morris household as 'Mac the Hack', shaped Mike's whole view of dentistry in Britain. As soon as he was old enough he ceased visiting the dentist and for the past ten years his teeth have remained unexposed. His total expectation is that of fear, anxiety and pain. However, as I frequently remind him, he is being small-minded and bigotted to which he agrees—but it has got him no nearer to the dentist. Fortunately, since moving to Chichester there is a fine lady dentist in the fellowship whom Mike respects and likes. It is possible in the not-too-distant future that he will put his trust in her assurances that dental care need not be a painful and negative experience and once again risk everything and place himself in 'the chair', submitting his molars for examination.

Amusing though such an account may appear, there is a very real principle of truth enshrined within it. We are all to one degree or another a product of our experiences. These have helped form our opinions and determine our expectations. Unfortunately in the area of the spiritual life, when we read the promises about answered prayer in the Bible we discover we are on the wrong side of a credibility gap because we have a long experience of unanswered prayer.

For years we have prayed: a good exam result for Tom (he failed), a successful visit to the doctor for Audrey (she's diagnosed as having cancer), sufficient finance for a holiday (nothing is forthcoming), a friend to be saved (they show no interest in the gospel) and so the list could go on. When our prayers appear unanswered we employ a mental conjuring trick, rapidly forgetting what we had been so earnestly praying for and beginning on something else for no other reason than the strict Christian injunction we were brought up on that we must pray. Is it really any wonder that calls to corporate prayer in our churches meet with such little enthusiasm? 95% of the congregation are living the experience of unanswered prayer and the fear that their poverty-stricken prayer life will one day in some way be revealed before the whole fellowship. Horrendous!

Obviously, none of us could continue with any integrity as disciples if we constantly lived with the tension of this credibility gap. So what we do is read the Bible on the one hand and subtly interpret it at the level of our experience. In essence we reduce what God has declared to fit our own experience of life and wear it as a coat that fits rather than keep it as a garment which is several sizes too large and apparently not for us. We may read a passage like 1 John 5:13-15—

> I am writing this to you so that you may know that you have eternal life—you that believe in the Son of God. We have courage in God's presence, because we are sure that he hears us if we ask him for anything that is according to his will. He hears us whenever we ask him; and since we know this is true, we know also that he gives us what we ask from him.

We then spend our time rationalizing the whole thing so that it no longer says what it appears to say at first reading, but something quite different which fits with our experience. Otherwise we concentrate on the phrase 'according to his will', and conclude we have nothing we pray for because it isn't in accord with his will. Quite

23

frankly, if as Christians we are incapable of discovering God's will we have little understanding of being born again of the Spirit of God. Furthermore, Scripture is a general revelation of God's will, part of which reveals that prayers are for the answering. It is interesting to note that no one would take a second glance at the phrase 'you may know that you have eternal life' because we are happy to accept it although we cannot prove it but only receive it by faith. Since eternity begins the day we meet Jesus, and one of the consequences of eternal life is God's will being done, how can we stumble over prayer in accordance with God's will and practical prayers receiving practical answers?

If that appears rather complicated do read it over again because it is essential to developing an effective prayer life. Consider the moment when you became a Christian. I don't know when that was, where that was or how that was. I had heard about Jesus and I went and discovered all the facts I could about this man and the claims that he had made. I learned about these things by reading the Bible and listening to Christian friends, and all that I heard confirmed to me that what Jesus claimed was true and could be effective for me. However, having said that, I could not discover if Jesus would meet with me until I risked everything and invited him to take over my life, till I said, 'I'm out of order and I need to get right with you, God.'

The illustration that most graphically depicts this for me is one where a child is standing at the top of a flight of stairs that lead down into a cellar. There is no light in the cellar and the child sees blackness. While the child is standing at the top of the stairs and looking down he hears a familiar voice. It is his father's voice and that voice says very simply, 'Jump.' Now the child's mind can reason that if the voice is that of his father, and he recognizes it to be so, then he can jump with confidence because Dad does not play nasty tricks upon him. Also if Dad is at the bottom of the stairs looking up, he can see his child because there is light behind the child even though the child cannot see down into the darkness of the cellar. However, the only way in which the child will ever know if the father will indeed catch him is if he fulfils the instruction to jump by jumping.

Similarly, in our Christian lives not one of us discovered whether the claims that Jesus had made about eternal life and friendship with God were true until we made that step of commitment, turned around and decided to give our lives to Jesus, to accept him as the boss. Only after praying some kind of prayer of commitment and meeting with Jesus did we discover that everything that we had assumed could be true was proven to be true in our experience.

So it is with our daily relationship with God. It is a relationship of faith in which we constantly have to leap from the top of those stairs into the arms of the one who loves us and whom we love. It is only once we've leaped into mid-air that we discover whether in fact God is going to catch us or let us crash into the concrete below and mockingly say, 'Fooled you.' This is not the heart and nature of the God we worship, so we can be confident that just as God has brought us to salvation, brought us into a relationship with himself, so he will continue to nurture, nourish and develop that relationship, for he wants good things for his children.

Instead of reducing God's word to the level of our experience, what I would like to suggest (and this is not an original thought) is that we alter our perspective and say, 'Lord, I see what your word says and I ask you to bring my life into line with your word.'

Imagine a pavement alongside which runs a three-foot-high wall. You are on the pavement and a friend is walking along the wall and you are holding hands with each other. Should you want to, you could very easily give your friend's hand a strong jerk and in no time at all he would be joining you on the pavement. However, you could decide to let your friend grip your hand strongly and, with your co-operation, haul you up onto the wall. Obviously it is far easier to pull your friend off the wall to pavement level than to be hauled up onto the wall. It is also evident that you would have a better perspective and panoramic view from the top of the wall than from the pavement.

This basically illustrates the choice that lies before us —the choice we will now need to take. Are we prepared to set aside past experience and ask God to bring our lives and future experience into line with his word? When Katey and I faced this we simply pictured God the Father standing by and offering us his hand. As he did this he invited us simply to place our hand in his hand and allow him to bring our life and experience into line with his word. It might help to picture this in the same way as you make your personal and yet practical response to God.

Consequences

As a couple, making such a practical response proved exceptionally helpful in stimulating our prayer life. The first time we decided to pray believing for specific and practical answers was in response to a news item on the radio. It revealed that a ferocious hurricane was heading directly for an island in some exotic spot and threatened to devastate it and its population entirely. There was neither the time nor the available resources to remove the population, and multiple deaths and severe injuries were forecast.

Horrified as we listened, Katey and I agreed to pray. We didn't know what to pray about but we simply asked God to save the island and its population from this expected destruction. This was done unemotionally and quickly, without much wailing and gnashing of teeth. From then on through the rest of the day we tuned in regularly for news of the hurricane's progress. Each time the voice of the newscaster clinically confirmed the worst fears of earlier bulletins—the island was facing a fatal encounter with an exceptionally violent storm.

As you can imagine, Katey and I felt full of doubt and very helpless, but we stuck to our guns, held on tightly to God's hand and quietly prayed again. I think each of us was constantly firing 'arrow prayers' to God on the island's behalf. In the late afternoon we listened to a further news report and learned to our surprise and joy that the hurricane had 'unaccountably' altered course at the last moment, veered away from the island and spent its force harmlessly in mid-ocean. God had heard our prayers and answered them. We were both greatly encouraged. On this issue our experience had come into line with God's word. Here was a practical, positive consequence from deciding to ask God to bring our lives into line with his word.

From that point on we have made it a principle rule to pray practically and specifically. However, we do not always see our prayers answered. There are issues for which we are praying which to this day remain unanswered; there are others which took a number of months before we enjoyed God's answer in reality; yet other situations met with immediate answers as in the case of the hurricane. The critical point is that for a number of years now we have continued to allow God to prove in concrete terms the truth of his word.

▶ Action stations

You were warned that this was a practical book on prayer. And so here's the place where you can get started. Find time—and now is the best time of all—to sit down with your partner and without any preliminaries pray together and out loud the Lord's Prayer:

> Our Father in heaven:
> May your holy name be honoured;
> may your Kingdom come;
> may your will be done on earth
> as it is in heaven.
> Give us today the food we need.
> Forgive us the wrongs we have done,
> as we forgive the wrongs that
> others have done to us.
> Do not bring us to hard testing,
> but keep us safe from the Evil One.

If you have not done so before, you have just prayed together. Now repeat the same but with eyes open, looking at each other and holding hands—there is nothing spiritual about shutting your eyes or adopting the 'shampoo position' for want of something to do with one's hands! Prayer is all about communication as we will see in the next chapter, and touch is essential to communication.

Finally, tonight before you go to bed pray again. Use the same prayer but this time pray alternate phrases so that while one speaks the other listens and then vice versa.

It wasn't so painful was it?

2

Praying Together Is Fun!

On my weekly trips to the Evangelical Alliance in London I have to take a bus from Victoria to Kennington. This is a tremendous eye-opener, or ear-opener I should say, when I both overhear and become involved in conversations ranging from the state of the weather to the state of the nation. My strangest encounter was with a bus conductor who was convinced that Hitler had been a guy with brilliant ideas whose only crime was to lose the war for which he had been punished with a poor press. It was worth considering that this conductor was not joking when he presented his political perspective to me.

About 90% of the people I overhear or chat to on a London bus are full of gloom and despondency. Life is a burden to be endured rather than enjoyed. Perhaps Alan Herbert was correct when he surmised, 'People must not do things for fun. We are not here for fun. There is no reference to fun in any act of parliament.'

It really concerns me that in a world sadly lacking in good news, those entrusted with the good news to end all news, namely the church of Jesus Christ—that is you and me, appear to be as burdened and impoverished as the world. Clive Calver speaks of a man he met after one service who, while shaking his hand, claimed that he had the joy of the Lord deep down inside. Such was his bearing and the sombre nature of his face that Clive reckoned it was so deep that it required three North Sea oil derricks to get it up to the surface!

So often everything associated with our worship of and work for God is sombre, dull and burdensome. The thought of praying or reading the Bible does not cause the heart to leap but rather to sink and groan. The very practice of all that we believe does not cause us to become overwhelmed with joy and excitement. It is hardly any wonder that the pagan already confronted with problems and pressures and convinced that the world is a place of gloom and doom, gives what he sees of Christianity a wide berth. However, I am convinced that God is a fun-loving God who 'generously gives us everything for our enjoyment' (1 Tim 6:17).

A relationship with Christ is for our enjoyment. I increasingly see God as fun-loving—getting excited and thrilled with the act of creation, setting stars spinning in their orbit, creating the animals. Surely God must have a sense of humour when you take a look at a camel! If that isn't sufficient, cast your eye on his pièce de resistance, that is man.

Many Christians have lost the twinkle in the eye, the sense of exhilaration and fun that God always intended for our relationship with him. Relationships depend upon humour, laughter and merriment otherwise they become cold and pragmatic. There is nothing sadder than a couple joined together through marriage who over the years have allowed the spark that drew them together to be extinguished, and while enjoying the legal status of being married, they have none of the life and spontaneity that enables the relationship to function. Many Christians hold in their hands the legal certificate of marriage to Christ, but any warmth and depth of relationship is all too soon replaced by a formal performance of expected duties.

Obviously this has serious implications for us in our prayer life, both as individuals and with each other. Prayer is ultimately about relationship. It is a means whereby we grow in our friendship and intimacy with God. It is the medium of communication between a people and their God and vice versa. When Moses went in to the presence of the Lord to chat things over, the relationship developed to the point that when he finally emerged he had to cover his face with a veil, such was the radiance of the Lord (Ex 34:29 ff). Indeed, Moses was the one with whom God spoke face to face (Num 12:6-8).

Choosing to relate to God

On reading through the Bible I am particularly struck by the character of Joshua. He is best known to us as the man who took over from Moses to lead Israel out of the wilderness and into the Promised Land. However, I find his personal spiritual journey before his appointment as Israel's leader most illuminating.

We first encounter Joshua in the book of Exodus where he is engaged in conflict with Israel's enemy the Amalekites (Ex 17:8 ff). The story is no doubt familiar. Joshua was directed by Moses to pick an army and engage the Amalekites in warfare. While Joshua battled in the field, Moses retreated with Aaron and Hur to a hill overlooking the skirmish and battled in prayer for victory. As long as Moses kept his hands in the air Joshua and the Israelites gained the upper hand, but when through tiredness Moses was forced to lower his hands the Amalekites seized the advantage in the conflict. Eventually, as the battle raged now one way and then the other, Aaron and Hur decided to hold Moses' hands in the air until sunset and so Joshua overcame the Amalekite army.

Imagine the scene following that victory, one that must have hung in the balance for the soldiers in the field. Tired but exultant the Israelites returned to their camp, maybe cheering their heroic leader Joshua. Naturally, those who had remained behind in the camp, aware that their destiny to some degree depended upon the success of their army, would have welcomed the men home with cheers and shouts, kisses and refreshments, and many would have directed special applause to Joshua their conquering captain in the fight.

At the best of times the Jews found it hard to fully appreciate Moses' leadership and were not above rebelling against it. This man raised by the Egyptians had a unique and awesome relationship with God. He was somewhat hard to relate to and identify with. But now they had a leader they could appreciate, a military man, a man of strength and vigour. You can almost see the mothers calculating how they might arrange a marriage for their daughter with this mighty man of valour—and I guess the dads weren't that far behind!

This was in fact a point of crisis for Joshua. He was a military man; he understood the dynamics of all that was taking place on the battlefield; he recognized that there was something more than military might behind the victory over the Amalekites that day. He realized that at times his army had been all but overwhelmed when suddenly the tables were turned, eventually so completely that the Israelites carried home the honours. I believe that as Joshua was cheered triumphantly back into the camp he caught sight of another small party who were entering the camp—Moses, Aaron and Hur. He saw the lines of exhaustion that marked Moses' face and he grasped the fact that while he had grappled with the Amalekites Moses had grappled with God, and between them faith and works had been combined to the glory of God and the benefit of Israel. Significantly, God required Moses to record this event in writing (Ex 17:14) and commanded him to ensure that Joshua personally heard the story of what he had done and what Moses had done that day. I would like to suggest that at this point Joshua, in the midst of personal adulation, determined to stick close to Moses and get to know this God who worked such powerful wonders. It was a costly decision because he had leadership offered to him on a plate by the celebrating army and camp.

My conjecture is supported from the very next appearance of Joshua in the Scriptures (Ex 24) when we learn that he is now Moses' assistant. Such was his determination to get to know this God whom Moses knew and who had given such a mighty victory, that he had settled for being Moses' servant—a step of some humility from the giddy heights of popular hero to unnoticed attendant. Significantly, it was Joshua and not Aaron and Hur who accompanied Moses up onto Mount Sinai when the covenant was confirmed and the glory of the Lord settled on the mountain. Joshua was growing in his relationship with God.

Joshua was prepared to make mistakes as well as to learn how to be God's man in a given situation (Num 11:28). It has been well said that someone who is not prepared to make a mistake will make nothing. In praying together, Katey and I have goofed and gaffed on numerous occasions. But the fruit of those mistakes has been growth in our understanding of God and of each other and a further insight into the nature and practice of prayer.

As we follow on with Joshua's growth in relationship with God, we discover that whenever Moses went out of the camp of the Israelites to consult with God in the tent of meeting, a place where God met with Moses face to face, Joshua would be close on his heels. Once Moses had done his business with God he would return to the camp, but Joshua did not leave the tent. Joshua learnt what it was to enjoy being with God. The Scriptures do not say that Joshua prayed or that God spoke to him, but we can assume that he enjoyed being in close proximity to God. Joshua learned to recognize when the presence of God was particularly close and he grew to love it and consider it worth remaining in the tent for.

One reason why we often fail to become excited by prayer is because we do not know what it is like to have God around. We know about him but we've not got very far down the road in relating to him. The Bible has a great word for describing this close relationship— 'abide'. Jesus used it in John 15 when he called his disciples to abide in him. It literally means to wait, to stay, to remain, to stand firm, to remain true to. Indeed, if we pause for just a moment and consider each of those meanings we get a very full and rich insight into what it means to be a friend of God.

It was while reading John 15 once that I discovered what Jesus was getting at when he said, 'Remain united to me, and I will remain united to you.' I knew just how good it was to have an evening at home with no one to see but Katey. The pleasure it was to prepare a good meal which could be taken at a leisurely pace. To put our feet up and either watch a film or listen to, say, a Bach violin concerto. We didn't need to speak but simply relish the fact that we were together and enjoyed being in each other's presence. Perhaps you can grasp more easily what I mean when I describe to you the isolation of returning home to an empty house, to get a meal for myself and spend an evening watching TV or listening to records alone. This was the situation when Katey was in hospital for ten days and I spent hours in the house on my own. Something was missing, or rather someone, and although I could work through the same pattern it was neither satisfying nor complete. This is why we need to discover everyday companionship with God and the emotional stability and security it brings.

Now I enjoy every moment of every day with God. When I walk the dog, for example, I enjoy God's companionship and we'll laugh together over many things. There are times when I am working flat out that I am reminded that God's around, and I push my chair back from the desk and take a few moments to appreciate what a friendship I have with the Lord. For his part he encourages me, gets me to laugh at myself, my mood or behaviour or just reminds me that I am his son and he thinks I am great. That's not big-headedness by the way, that's the Bible!

Learning to appreciate God can cause a certain amount of embarrassment. I well remember walking the dog around our local golf-course one morning, singing aloud and generally getting very excited at how big God is and yet how personal and practical his love for us is. My mind recalled two or three areas of anxiety that Katey and I had faced which we had eventually (note not immediately because we are slow learners too) prayed about and consequently seen resolution to our great relief. As I chatted with God on my walk, thanking him for this, I was literally filled to overflowing with gratitude and excitement, and as I sang aloud I began to leap around and dance up the fairway. Landing gracefully from a well-executed pirouette I saw someone on the green observing me.

I focused upon them and recognized the steward who was placing the flags in their holes. He looked absolutely stunned and as I resumed a more decorous form of progress towards this same green, giving a friendly wave as I went, he hurriedly disappeared towards his next port of call somewhat perplexed if not a little concerned at what he had observed. Still, I am not the first to be observed 'walking and jumping and praising God' (Acts 3:8)!

On recalling that scenario I can still sense my own embarrassment at the time, caught out as it were in my private devotions. And probably rightly embarrassed because I was communicating the intimacy with my God. I have learned that relating to God involves not only the mind but also the emotions, and certainly as I have broken through emotional barriers such as dance I have discovered a new level of closeness with the Lord himself. We all face a number of personal issues as we develop an active and effective prayer life and each of us will have to decide whether we will face these and press through them. Let's take a few that affect us as couples learning to pray together.

Embarrassment

I have looked at this briefly from a personal point of view but this is also a major area for us as a couple. Somehow it felt silly and unreal saying, 'Let's pray together.' As we adopted our prayerful position, an unhelpful tension and religiosity seemed to overtake us. The voices we used to chat things over with each other assumed an unnatural holy tone and the whole thing was awful. I usually emerged grumpy and critical and poor Katey quietly endured the whole procedure, believing this must be the pain of submission to your husband!

What was even more horrendous was that we were unable to talk the problems through because we wouldn't admit to each other that it was awful.

So all that happened was that we prayed less and less together, lived under a burden of guilt because we weren't a praying couple and when the guilt became intense, set a whole evening aside to pray (to pull back some brownie points on God's great prayer ledger) which was always a disaster. After all, if you can't pray together effectively for ten minutes why should you be able to pray for two hours?

We only began to get this sorted out once we realized that it was false to assume that we knew how to pray simply because we had been told to pray from the moment we had been converted. We had to admit our inadequacy to God and to each other in this department of our lives. We then had to begin to practice being natural in prayer as we were natural in having lunch together, doing the shopping together or walking in the country together. Like Jesus' disciples we came hand in hand and said, 'Teach us to pray,' and from a position of ignorance we began to learn.

▶ *Action stations*

Get together with your partner and take a few minutes, one after the other, to pray out of your love for the other. For example, Katey usually uses the illustration of how she would thank God for my smile by praying, 'Thank you Lord for the smile that you have given Mike, that it is so broad and lights up his whole face. Thank you that he smiles so often and that it is often directed towards me.' You'll find this a heart-warming exercise and full of fun, so enjoy yourselves together.

Tension

Having agreed to do this a whole new area of difficulty opened up. We needed to be real, i.e. honest with each other, and if there is one thing guaranteed to make sparks fly in any marriage it's when your partner tells you a few home truths. However, we were to discover that it was impossible to enjoy God together if we weren't totally honest with each other.

Katey vividly remembers our early attempts to pray together. I would read a passage from the Bible and before praying enter on a long exposition for Katey's benefit. All the while she was sitting there with a demure look on the outside but inside thinking, 'I can do without all this. I know what God has said to me so why can't we cut the sermon?' Once I had finished my homily was it any wonder that prayer fell flat with me expecting some kind of response from Katey while she resented my arrogance in preaching at her. It was a long time before Katey gently told me to 'shut up!'. Being a reasonable fellow I responded by storming out of the room. Such are the delights of marriage!

Once I cooled off I had to admit that Katey was right. This obviously gave her greater courage because she then went on to explain that not only was I preaching at her but assuming a voice reminiscent of a foghorn to do so. I felt quite threatened and sensitive by this assault on what Katey dubs my 'preaching voice', but we had to work through it. Hardest of all was for 'macho Mike' to admit this sense of threat and hurt produced by Katey's honesty.

If we are going to progress in prayer as couples we will have to face and work through the threat we pose to each other and give room for honest criticism and positive response.

▶ *Action stations*

Get together with your partner. Each of you will need a sheet of paper and a pencil. Now what you must do is write down three strengths that you recognize in your partner. Don't talk, just write.

Once you have written these down, and do take a moment or two to think what you will write, share with each other what you have written down. Men must share first.

Now, having done that write down three weaknesses you recognize in your partner.

Once you have written them down, share again. This time women share first.

This is a lovely way of being able to be honest with each other and we have seen such an exercise bring about real reconciliation between couples.

Remember the purpose of such an exercise is to take some real steps forward in being relaxed and open with each other, so don't neglect to do this regularly with each other. In the next chapter we will look at why men shared the strengths first and women the weaknesses.

Faithlessness

As we've mentioned previously, many of us continue to pray with a long-standing testimony of unanswered prayer. The fruit of this is that we are to all intents and purposes faithless. We do not expect God to act in answer to our prayers, so we perform our duty of prayer but it is no more than a dreary duty. Unfortunately we are not helped here by twentieth-century rationality that can only conceive of things happening if they lie within the parameters of our mental understanding. However, the Bible reveals that God is someone who acts the moment we stop relying on human resources to perform the tasks.

Take the story of the rich young ruler in Matthew 19:16-30. Challenged by his disciples over the impossibility of a rich man entering the kingdom of heaven, Jesus responds, 'This is impossible for man, but for God everything is possible' (Mt 19:26). For us this implies that the moment we exhaust the realm of the humanly possible, God sweeps in and turns our impossibility into his glorious possibility.

For example, when we were going to get married we wanted to buy a house. We were living in Wolverhampton, and friends who were moving offered us their house at £1,000 below the market value. We needed a mortgage. Katey was a teacher with a regular wage, but I had no guaranteed salary. Every building society we approached viewed us as a potential calamity financially and were unable to help. Somewhat discouraged we returned to the BYFC office where I worked and let Clive Calver know our predicament. In characteristic fashion he said, 'What we need here is a miracle,' prayed and sent us out to try another building society. As you may have guessed, this society welcomed us with open arms and gave us a mortgage three times Katey's salary with no guaranteed income from myself.

I learned a lot that day, not least from Clive, about God meeting us at the point at which we exhaust human means and literally taking hold of the impossible and bringing it into existence. This principle is not one by which we can guarantee personal financial prosperity, it is a principle that God moves in response to believing men and women.

▶ *Action stations*

We can encourage each other greatly in building faith

into one another's lives.

Get together again and with a piece of paper and pencil each, write down something about which you want to receive an answer from God. It does not need to be in the material realm. It might be in the area of spiritual development, or it might have to do with an opportunity to speak to a friend or relation. Now, once you have both written something down, join hands and with your free hand hold up the paper to God and ask him to respond to your request.

Do be realistic about what you are asking of God, and remember you are laying building-blocks for growing closer to God and enlarging your faith.

One example of when I followed this practice was the time when Clive and I, having appointed a new secretary, needed to furnish her with a decent typewriter. I told God all about it and then went ahead and placed the order—the total price was £600. It was the day before the bill needed to be paid, and no £600 had appeared. Clive and I were returning from a meeting and we pulled into a service station for petrol. Having filled up I looked down at my feet to discover a £20 note. Bending down to pick it up I found another, then another and finally a thick wad of notes. I put them in my pocket, feeling I was more trustworthy than the petrol attendant.

On returning home we informed the police of the find and they told us to keep the money in the BYFC account while we waited to see if anyone would claim it. After six months no one had, and so the money became the property of the finder, that was BYFC. The total amount? Well, £600 of course—the price of the new typewriter!

If we will co-operate with God we will daily discover that man's impossibilities provide the doorways to God's possibilities. So let's get on with it!

Don't be afraid to go back over the 'Action Stations'

sections and repeat them. The whole point of the exercise is to become natural and at ease in praying together, not just to complete the tasks.

3
Let's Talk About It

Any relationship is dependent for its survival on communication. This is true for every marriage partnership and every relationship between an individual and God.

Throughout the Old Testament God communicated repeatedly with his wayward people Israel to encourage them and correct them and to remind them that they were married to him and therefore had an exclusive relationship with him and he with them. Their disobedience became so great that God refused to speak for 300 years until he made his final statement. This was his Son Jesus. Hebrews 1:1-2 states,

> In the past, God spoke to our ancestors many times and in many ways through the prophets, but in these last days he has spoken to us through his Son. He is the one through whom God created the universe, the one whom God has chosen to possess all things at the end.

That communication between God and his people continues today; his people now being those who know and love Jesus, who have an exclusive attachment to him as he has to them. That communication is vital for the maintenance and development of the relationship between the disciple and God.

Unfortunately, just as communication between a Christian and his God can fall into disrepair and neglect with the stagnation of their relationship, the same can happen between man and wife in marriage. This is a tragedy whenever and wherever it occurs. There is an unspoken assumption today that marriage somehow happens—we are merely passive partners who enjoy the fruit of the relationship. If there is little fruit it is time to change partners, establish a new marriage. The fault is with the marriage not with us. It is little wonder that nationally one in three marriages end in divorce, a figure which according to recent reports will soon increase to one in two. Those of us within the church, however, have little room for complacency or outrage since the failure rate here is reputed to be one in five.

Now I appreciate marriage is no easy matter. We are involved with the premarital counselling of many young couples and few can get their eyes beyond the wedding day and the wedding night! That's no surprise, and it's encouraging that they have such a sense of anticipation. However, unless they can appreciate that the wedding day is just the beginning of a long, exciting and arduous journey, they will make inadequate preparations for encountering the obstacles which may lie before them in the course of their marriage.

The day Katey and I got married was a great day. We were glad when it arrived since the months running up to the wedding were a time of hassle and pressure. The arrangements for the wedding, responding rightly to the families, seeking to prevent the physical relationship from running away with itself (with all the emotional pressure of the wedding the security and stability we found in each other over that period heightened the

44

physical tension).

The day itself, July 29th 1978 (a date later recognized for its quality and utilized by the Prince and Princess of Wales for their nuptial celebration), was boiling hot and filled with excitement. Katey felt hotter than the rest since she had a temperature of 100°, not she assures me at the thought of marrying my good self, but as a result of flu. Everything went fairly well—apart from forgetting to lift Katey's veil at the appropriate moment, so leaving her to swelter still further, and the organist striking up the tune 'While shepherds watched their flocks by night' for the hymn 'O for a thousand tongues to sing'. Strange experience! The service over, it was great to have all the attention of the cameras, making speeches at the reception, saying cheerio to everyone and then clanking off down the road into a lifetime of married bliss.

It was only after the wedding day that reality set in. Seated across the table from Katey at breakfast, I'd ask myself where was that radiant personification of feminine beauty who had swept up the aisle to be joined in matrimony to me? And why was it that piles of junk collected at inappropriate places around the house? And did my trousers really require three creases? Katey of course was contemplating a similar series of thoughts. When would the washer on the tap get replaced? Did I have to pick my nose so publicly? Did we always have to watch war films?

Indeed, the source of greatest frustration between us in the early days of marriage was my nose-picking and the way Katey ate an apple. Pitiful issues, but they assumed great importance to us. And we were poor at communicating in a reasonable way. I'm convinced that communication, or rather lack of it, is a major factor in marriage problems today. It wasn't long before we realized that marriage did not serve us but we have to serve or service it. There was no place for passivity—we had to work actively at relating together. In doing so we learned a number of valuable lessons about communication which have since enhanced our marriage to each other and our friendship with God.

The most important lesson was that what I thought I said was apparently not what Katey heard. For example, Katey turns on the TV. Observing the programme I say, 'I can't stand this!' Katey hears my words but interprets them as, 'I shouldn't have put the TV on,' or, 'How dare he criticize my choice of programme. I have a right to relax too.' Instantly, Katey is grumpy. I get a few atmospherics from the good lady and find myself developing feelings of criticism and alienation towards her for no apparent reason. Result—a rotten evening which has to be worked through before retiring to fulfil the scriptural injunction, 'Do not stay angry all day' (Eph 4:26).

Many were the nights we sat up and talked long and hard in the first year of our marriage; resolving conflicts and misunderstandings; learning to express the way in which we felt hurt by the other and finding a creative and positive way forward. It was only slowly that we discovered that sometimes what we intended to communicate was not reflected to the other by the words we chose. We had to ensure we had been understood, and also provide room for the response of the other, a response that could be positive or negative, without further reaction on either of our parts.

We had to learn to be direct in what we said and not abuse our relationship by seeking to manipulate it. On my part this entailed not taking unilateral decisions and dumping them and their consequences lock, stock and barrel, without giving Katey the right of reply. And for Katey's part, not seeking to choose her moment and line of approach to get round me but rather to state clearly and directly what she was getting at. Many are the games we play in marriage, but the manipulation game should not be one of them. Marriage is a partnership of equals, and as with every partnership the everyday detailed practice needs working at. It is not healthy when we discover ways in which we can achieve our desires and ends through sly manipulation of our partner.

It has been our experience that learning to communicate effectively takes time and energy but pays rich dividends. After eight years of marriage we have not adjusted to each other but become knit together as one, each readjusting where necessary. We have had to learn that we need to take as much care about how we express ourselves as what we express. Previously one of us might have communicated something that was true but presented it in completely the wrong way. Result? A local nuclear explosion of unseemly proportions, in the midst of which the truism was entirely lost. With a little thought and a sense of timing, that which needed to be said could have been outlined without an adverse reaction and with sufficient grace for the issue to be talked through.

This lesson has been vital to our relationship, for in the early days Katey lived in fear of my hot and fiery temper. This had such an effect upon her that she would take virtually any action to avoid stirring me up. The consequence was that areas in my own life which radically required the firm application of the boot were left to continue and fester. Katey was too fearful to challenge me, and I was utilizing my hot temper to keep her and virtually anyone else from levelling with me. I didn't realize it at the time, but I was of course the loser missing out on God transforming my character and making me more like Jesus.

After a number of difficult years, we at last began to

communicate a little more honestly and easily as out-lined above. I gave Katey the right, and requested that she took the responsibility, to tell me when I was being a selfish pig or when I was over-reacting, etc. The immedi-ate consequences of this were that Katey, summoning up all her courage would challenge me and I would refuse to receive what she said. However, I knew I was out of order, and so in our many reconciliations I asked her to forgive me.

We then turned to prayer. I asked God's forgiveness and asked Katey to pray for me. The fruit was that I began to be able to hear her words without over-reacting, and trust her judgements, given for my benefit and out of her love for me. The long-term fruit is that I am now a better adjusted individual: I trust and value Katey's 'input' into my life; I depend upon her keeping a critical eye on my life and my ministry, and I am so much more secure in myself and therefore less vulnerable when with other people and willing to receive honest comment from them. Katey and I are the richer for this. It is a process that we have each had to grow through, and continue to do so, recognizing that it is vital if we are to be effective partners.

Appreciate you are different

Charles Dickens, it is said, had a particularly unhappy marriage, eventually remaining joined to his wife in holy matrimony by word only. In speaking of this unhappy relationship he recalled how once he expressed his in-tention to marry, many of his friends urged him to recon-sider on the grounds that they could see great trouble ahead for such a fiery couple. In spite of the warnings and as well as the constant in-fighting between Charles and his bride-to-be, the wedding took place, the marriage was entered into. It was soon evident to both husband and wife that marriage of itself did not remove any of the problems and difficulties experienced during courtship, and indeed Dickens coined the phrase that rather than reducing areas of conflict, marriage 'magnifies problems'.

This insight—marriage magnifies problems—is absolutely fundamental. Knowing this to be true we can take positive action in response. We begin by recognizing that men are different from women—bright boy you may say, you knew that all along. But, have we really learned to appreciate how different the sexes are, and learned to build with those differences in mind?

The day before our first wedding anniversary we went through the worst crisis of our married life to date. We were having breakfast with friends and I was in the middle of retelling what I thought was a very amusing joke. As I built towards the punchline, Katey leaped in and in a rather pedantic and mocking way pre-empted me with the punchline. At that moment I felt belittled in front of our friends, totally insecure and thoroughly betrayed. Without thinking I responded by throwing the contents of a freshly made, boiling hot cup of coffee all over Katey. With the shock and the heat she rushed out of the kitchen in tears, I immediately regretted what I'd done and felt more stupid than ever, and our friends made a wise and discreet departure. I sought out Katey upstairs, nursing somewhat reddened flesh and began the process of apology and reconciliation. To this day that incident is etched on my mind and still causes me to feel ashamed when I consider it.

In that incident Katey had trodden on the male ego and I had reacted most violently. In our discussions following that incident we began to discover that the make-up of a man is very different from that of a woman.

Think back, if you will, to the exercise in the last chapter where you each identified strengths and weaknesses in each other (page 39). You will recall that when you identified strengths in each other we insisted that men share first. The reason for this is that women are often starved of encouragement. For so long social conditioning has directed women towards a role of subservience that they seldom exercise their gifts and abilities to the full. Therefore husbands have an important role in identifying strengths and abilities in their wives, encouraging them and enabling them to practise and develop such gifts. Too often as guys we overlook the creative touches and very real capabilities in our wives, and fail to provide the nurture they require.

Katey and I are convinced that there appears to be such a dearth of female leadership within the church because even where we have rejected an ecclesiology that relegates women to the role of spectators not participators, we have failed to engage in a programme of providing positive, practical opportunities for women to exercise their gifts. In our marriages, as we firstly encourage our wives through identification of gifts, and secondly provide the practical environment of prayer together for the exercise of those gifts, we can help prepare a whole host of women for leadership roles, for taking over areas of responsibility within the church and society generally. At a time when the feminist agenda is up for discussion, we have the opportunity to demonstrate God's creative perspective through the church.

I first recognized the need for active encouragement for Katey when I discovered she would often 'put herself down' in company or excuse something which simply did not need excusing. As I travelled the country I discovered that this was a common occurrence among the ladies in whose homes I enjoyed hospitality, and that their husbands often seemed unaware of it. The clearest example I can recall occurred over meals. Whenever we entertained, which was frequently, I could guarantee that whatever Katey served up, which was always admirable, she would apologize for, or at least for some part of it. I encountered this same attitude in home after home as meals were set before me. My response was simple; I began to thank Katey for her choice of menu, the quality of the meal and the little touches she had included in setting the table, such as a small vase of fresh flowers as a table decoration. It was glorious to see her flourish under this encouragement and also to develop a greater confidence in hospitality, a subject about which she is now well able to speak on the couples' weekends that we are involved in.

This same principle of encouragement has allowed Katey to develop a speaking role in her own right, rather than shelter behind me and just pop up with the occasional illustration. As husbands we must encourage our wives so that they can fulfil their potential in God. So be a practical encourager.

In the 'Action Stations' exercise in chapter 2 we said that when it comes to identifying weaknesses it is the ladies who should speak first. Often wives know more about their husbands than the husbands realize. Suffice it to say that we men are egotists, with an ego which longs to be applauded and acknowledged.

Wives need to become an anchor point for husbands, and as husbands we need to learn to make room for our wives' valuable input in areas of weakness. We meet so many men who exercise positions of leadership in church life but whose character has sadly never kept pace with the development of their gift. Can there be a sadder sight than a man, mature in years, unable to respond to criticism in any other way than anger? Wives are a godsend because they can actually build character into the lives of their husbands by challenging the weaknesses and precipitating the necessary crises for these weaknesses to be dealt with. Husbands have to develop the humility necessary for this to happen, wives the boldness mixed with much wisdom.

Obviously, wives need their own weaknesses to be identified too, and husbands need encouragement. But it is our experience that encouragement is the place for husbands to start with their wives and weaknesses the place for wives to start with husbands. Of course, none of this can work outside of the security of our relationship with God, and so highlights another vital reason why we must begin to pray together effectively.

Marriage in 3D

In concluding this chapter I want to express our conviction that marriage is supported on three foundational pillars: the social dimension, the sexual dimension and the spiritual dimension. Remove any one of those pillars and a marriage becomes one third more liable to fail to function effectively or even to fail altogether.

The social dimension

When a couple enter into marriage they often assume that they are totally sufficient for each other, so previous friendships are often dropped and very quickly the couple only have one another to socialize with. This is tragic. Katey and I quickly discovered we were not socially sufficient for one another. She still needed to meet up with her girlfriends and do things with them. Likewise I would meet up with my mates for the occasional evening or go off for a day to a sporting fixture or some such event. Furthermore, we needed to develop relationships together with other couples—folk to share holidays with or weekends away. We also discovered that we quickly developed friendships together with single folk, our home becoming an open home. This would mean that I would spend more time with the single fellows on various outings, Katey with the girls, as well as the time we spent together.

We found that very quickly you can get stuck in a rut in marriage and as someone once said, the only difference between a rut and a grave is about 5 feet. We had to be creative about the way we used time off together. Rotting in front of the TV was a dead end. Therefore we began to walk together and explore places. We have recently joined the National Trust so that we can pop into gardens and houses of historic interest and enjoy ourselves in this way. We joined with a good friend and wrote into our diaries weekends visiting various locations. All three of us recently visited Petworth House near where we live and had a really good, relaxing and refreshing day chatting and enjoying each other's company. On a recent speaking engagement Katey and I popped out during the afternoon off and visited some lovely gardens. We were able to reflect on the weekend of ministry and plan for the rest of our time there in the most beautiful and restful of surroundings. So many couples lose this social dimension, only to discover that their relationship turns stale and that they are drifting apart.

This social dimension is absolutely essential and quite possible to maintain. If you are broke financially you need to become creative. Over a period when Katey and I were at our poorest we still found social outgoings. We turned a trip to the opticians (for free eye-tests) into a real day out, and what's more had a very fruitful time of conversation with the Hindu optician.

If you are surrounded by children include them in. I am for ever indebted to my parents who always found something for us to do as a family of five each weekend. We had no car so we would be walked up to the park to feed the ducks, visit the children's zoo, play cricket or hide-and-seek. These form some of my happiest childhood memories, and having since been responsible for entertaining young children I appreciate the effort and cost my mum and dad were prepared to make.

In a recent edition of *Chat* I was struck by the title of an article, 'The family that eats together stays together.'

Identifying something rapidly disappearing from life in our society, the family meal, the paper recognized that family breakdown may well be increased through failure to function as a family. The same is true for couples minus the children as well.

The sexual dimension

The second pillar supporting the marriage is in the sexual sphere. It has been said that if you put a coin in a jar every time you made love in the first year of your marriage you'd spend the rest of your years emptying the jar! Unfortunately there is a grain of truth in this statement. For many couples sex falls into disuse in their marriage as they advance in years. Yet sex is an essential and vital ingredient in every marriage. Paul himself wrote, 'Do not deny yourselves to each other, unless you first agree to do so for a while in order to spend your time in prayer; but then resume normal marital relations. In this way you will be kept from giving in to Satan's temptation because of your lack of self-control' (1 Cor 7:5).

The marriage bed is the place where we learn to lose our inhibitions towards each other, the place where we learn to relax together and laugh together. For all those couples who have puffed and panted their way through various sexual activities the words of St Francis in describing the human body as 'brother Ass' will cause a degree of mirth and agreement. Much is to be learned through our sexual exploits together. The need to give and not to take, to put one's partner's pleasure first, to be unembarrassed in showing one's partner what pleases and to talk honestly and naturally. The learning experience of investigating new positions can be a source of much amusement if not potential physical injury.

Katey and I have discovered that our sexual relationship has grown over the years and benefited through positive communication and learning to be fully relaxed with each other. If you can become totally uninhibited and honest in bed together this encourages and ensures a level of honest communication which services the marriage. It also produces a sense of oneness and dependence which works actively against falling into sexual immorality. Tony Campolo maintained that the average person falls in love seven times before they get married and seven times after they get married! Once you've stopped counting for yourself, remember there are plenty of attractive men and women in the world and none of us is above being tempted into adultery. A positive sexual relationship together as couples is a good protection for our marriages; and if we learn to be at ease with each other then we can express to our partners those members of the opposite sex we find attractive without threatening them. This again acts as a useful deterrent against immorality. Katey knows who I find attractive and I know which male has the sexiest backside as far as Katey is concerned!

The spiritual dimension

So to the final pillar—that which is perhaps best recognized and least practised. The Catholics have coined the

55

phrase, 'The family that prays together stays together,' and there is a great element of truth in that. I love visiting homes of families where prayer is obviously such a natural part of their life together that the children are not in the least nonplussed by it. While staying with one family recently, grace was sung to the tune of 'Thank you very much', obviously a home-grown family version—excellent!

The most difficult nettle to grasp is the tyranny of 'ought'. We all know we ought to pray but don't know how to. The initial thing to do is to sit down and determine when you are going to get started and then start at that agreed point. We shall look at this in the next chapter.

Prayer, like the social and the sexual, provides yet another forum in which we can relate. It includes God much more actively than the other two areas. It is a time for airing hurts and grievances, joys and expectations, and receiving support and encouragement from our partners in the name of God. Katey and I have known anxiety replaced by peace, anger replaced by love and fragmentation replaced by reconciliation as we have prayed together. Indeed, in times of pressure we now actively seek God first of all rather than allowing ourselves to be chewed up by our immediate circumstances. We have also developed a respect and confidence in each other's ability to minister Jesus and have benefited greatly from the practical application of the same.

We will now move on to how we get started, but don't forget our relationships need to function on the social, the sexual and the spiritual planes.

▶ *Action stations*

Get together as couples with pencil and paper handy.

Answer the following questions honestly by writing your responses on your paper.

Social dimension:
   (1) Do I have personal friends with whom I spend time at work
       at home
       elsewhere?
   (2) As a couple am I happy with how we use our leisure time?
   (3) Would I like to entertain in our home more often?

Sexual dimension:
   (1) Do I feel relaxed enough with my partner to tell him/her how he/she could give me greater pleasure sexually?
   (2) Am I happy that we make love regularly enough?
   (3) Would I be able to tell my partner if I found someone else attractive?

Spiritual dimension:
   (1) Do I want to pray with my partner regularly?
   (2) What is the greatest single factor preventing me from praying with my partner?
   (3) Would the children be embarrassed by family prayers?

Now talk through your answers together.

4
Plotting Our Course and Setting Sail

It was said, a little unkindly, of Christopher Columbus, the great explorer who rediscovered America, that he set out not knowing where he was going, arrived not knowing where he was and returned not knowing where he had been—and the whole lot on borrowed money! An entrepreneur of some standing!

For many of us this has been our experience of prayer together. We have faithfully cast off, not quite knowing where precisely we are aiming for. We fire off a few prayers this way and that and finally land, full of dissatisfaction. We then quietly forget about praying together and make out as best we can without it. And what of the borrowed money? Well, we are often stirred into action following a couple's testimony or yet another call to prayer or a wave of guilt, hence acting on someone else's prayer experience instead of investing in one of our own. However, we can all begin our own account at any time and invest in it regularly together.

Before we achieve anything we need to know where we are heading and how we intend to get safely to our destination. Once as a teenager on holiday in Bournemouth I hired a rowing-boat and set off out to sea. I had no idea of where I was going to row to and did not have a watch to tell me the time. I rowed and rowed, thoroughly enjoying the vigorous exercise and letting my imagination have full range—one moment escaping pirates, the next smuggling contraband across the water under the noses of the king's men. I was eventually brought back to reality when I was hailed by a passing yacht. The skipper enquired if I was in need of assistance since they were not used to meeting rowing-boats so far out, but I cheerily said I was fine. Then I realized the pier and coastline were really quite small. Obviously my rowing, aided by the ebbing tide, had carried me a good distance from the shore. I turned the boat about and began the long row in, pausing every so often to peer over my shoulder and get a bearing on the pier for which I was aiming. Three hours—and a pair of very weary arms—later I made shore to be greeted by a rather irate boatman who informed me that he shut at five o'clock (it was now gone six!) and that I had only hired the boat for a two-hour period. I apologized, negotiated a realistic price for my total hiring and went off to find somewhere to get food and drink. The abiding memory is that rowing is not for me and a somewhat jaundiced view of boating generally.

Had I planned properly I could have had a very pleasant afternoon's boating instead of that nightmare—and for many of us this is true of our prayer life. A series of poor experiences prevents us from getting our act together effectively. Katey and I meet so many couples who, in trying to pray together, have set aside a large chunk of time and emerged thoroughly depressed by it— it has been uninspiring and exceptionally boring, and what's more they missed their favourite TV programme. Sacrificing something for God which leaves one feeling disgruntled strikes me as bad news.

We started to add a spiritual dimension to our marriage in a very small way about two years after our wedding. We had both been given copies of *Living Light* on the occasion of our baptisms, and one night we decided to read the verses set aside for that date. It really was no more than reading them through before putting the light out. At the time Katey was teaching in a rather difficult school and one night asked if we could pray about some problem she had to face the following day. Surprisingly enough it worked and we would pray whenever either of us faced a situation needing divine intervention. This developed into a longer time and we decided that perhaps it would be more suitable if we spent time together at the beginning of the day. This we did and also introduced Bible readings. It was not a particularly long time spent in deep Bible study and prayer, but it was a start. *Living Light* had been a good starting-point, providing a loose structure we could easily fit into and eventually leading to Bible reading and prayer at the start of the day.

When we did finally manage to establish a regular, enjoyable and effective prayer life it was only by observing some very basic ground rules.

1. Be practical

So often we imagine we will drift in and out of prayer without a second thought. While I recognize that I am not the most organized of people and Katey probably less so, it soon became evident that unless we took one simple decision our prayer life together would remain in tatters. So the first question we asked each other was, 'When shall we pray?' Initially this was for us last thing at night. Because we made it a priority we achieved it even when tired. Once Katey gave up work we established a time at the start of the day—a nice breakfast together in the company of Radio 4's *Today* programme, or Radio 3's selection, followed by prayer. We noticed an amazing difference once we settled on a time.

Having chosen the time when we would pray, we then agreed on how long we would pray for. Initially we spent ten minutes last thing at night. This grew to around half an hour maximum—a time span we only occasionally extend. We discovered it better to pray effectively for ten minutes than struggle through forty-five minutes of tedium and frustration.

Once we had established the time and the duration, we would take a couple of minutes at the start to identify the people and situations for which we would pray. It's surprising how often our mind goes a complete blank when we start praying. Once we had three or four items for prayer we got on with it. We soon learned not to be anxious if we each prayed for the same person or situation one after the other, or if other previously unmentioned items got incorporated. Our agreed time over we'd finish and go to sleep. We felt really chuffed that we had prayed, fulfilled our target and established a pattern.

▶ *Action stations*

Together decide when you will pray and for how long you will pray. Be realistic. Start small and leave room for growth. Having made your agreement decide when will be the first day you put your decision into action.

2. Be disciplined

One of the rare scientific facts I learned at school (I once scored a miserable $8/100$ for a physics paper!) was that a vacuum was a void incapable of supporting life. Unfortunately many of us create a vacuum when we pray together. We adopt the aforementioned 'shampoo position', a holy hush descends and then . . . nothing! Maybe a few mutterings of 'Thank you, Jesus' or a sigh or two, but apart from these nothing.

I well remember when we started praying I would launch out into an all-embracing theological epic and end with a solid 'Amen'. I would then think inwardly, 'Katey, now it's your turn.' Silence reigned. I continued to think Katey ought to get on with it and still she didn't. Then I twigged. Obviously Katey must be in sin and struggling to find the words for a suitable confession. Well I'd wait, and following her confession minister the grace and forgiveness of God (see what I mean about the male ego mentioned in the last chapter?). Still not a word from Katey. Not only was she in deep sin, she must be in outright rebellion as well. This was a task for super-Christian—in other words, me. So with a good dose of condemnation I'd challenge Katey who had been quietly enjoying the Lord and trying to keep in touch with my initial extended prayer, and immediately put her back up. Unable to back down, the prayer time would halt and we would depart our separate ways, grumpy, frustrated and out of fellowship with each other.

We came to learn that our times of prayer needed a helmsman, someone to give a bit of guidance when the going was getting nowhere. We began to break in on the silences by suggesting the other might like to pray for one of the items we had listed, or read a scripture for meditation and then request feedback. It was evident that our times of prayer required a disciplined direction and we each had a responsibility for ensuring this took place. Katey asked if I would carry the ultimate responsibility for this as she preferred not to.

The fruit of all this was that I would act as a sort of chairman and provide a running commentary as and when necessary. If there was silence I would say, 'Let's concentrate upon God's grace for the next two minutes and then give thanks for what we've gained,' or, 'Let's take the next three minutes praying for those we know who are being persecuted,' or, 'Let's bombard God with a stream of short, sharp prayers of thanksgiving' etc. This immediately removed any sense of tension or uncertainty that had accompanied our prayer life together and gave it a very positive framework in which to grow.

▶ Action stations

Take time to decide who will carry the ultimate responsibility for keeping your prayer times moving forward in a positive and disciplined direction. Having made your decision, act upon it and stick to it.

3. Be honest

I don't know how many of you have been in those prayer meetings where in the guise of talking to God an individual really communicates what they want to say to somebody else in the prayer group. Frankly, it is one of the most despicable abuses of a time of prayer to have a go at someone under the apparent safety of talking to God. I'm sure God finds this detestable. It may be hard to face up to people with issues, but it's something we have to learn. And it's something we can learn a lot about in the context of praying together.

We are not to abuse prayer by lecturing each other 'in the name of Jesus, Amen'. We are not to pray, for example, 'Lord, I pray that you will deal with Mary's temper. It is obviously an offence to you and no help to her.

Please remove Mary's temper and give her your grace and patience.' As Mary sits and listens to this she is immediately out of fellowship with God and with you. Have the gumption to talk about temper together, not through the medium of prayer. If it is an issue then encourage Mary to have it dealt with through ministry and prayer. Together you can build a framework which will help Mary avoid situations which cause her to lose her temper. You might discover you are a most frustrating character to share the same house with and need to put your own house in order as well. Painful stuff this praying together, but the raw material for effective marriage relationships.

This ability to be able to confront without ultimate offence is essential. I say ultimate offence because in the first instance if I am confronted I will most likely overreact. However, in the fullness of time I will see the error of my ways, the truth of that with which I was confronted and I will want to deal with the situation. If we can learn to do this in the intimacy of our marriage relationships we will become a better person to live with, exercise a greater level of maturity within the body of Christ—able to receive and respond to constructive criticism and encouragement—and a valuable resource to the church in discipling and pastoring others. Sad to say, many in Christian leadership are prepared to demand a level of submission in others which they would never be prepared to receive themselves.

Another issue which surfaced once we started praying together was that of criticism. For no apparent reason I would find myself becoming irritated with Katey over ridiculous things—her prayers, the tone of her voice, the things she forgot to pray. Indeed, I found myself listening intently to every word and missing the purpose of prayer altogether.

There's a story told of a young man who was converted and came from a rough background who was brought along to the mid-week prayer meeting. He found himself in a world he barely recognized. People praying interminably in a language which he thought had died with Shakespeare. However, wishing to communicate with God he opened his mouth and talked with his heavenly Father, briefly and in a language with which he was comfortable. The prayer meeting over he was approached by one of the leaders of the church and taken on one side. He was informed that his prayer was a little inappropriate and not quite what the prayer meeting was used to. Thinking for a moment he replied, 'Well, I wasn't talking to you, I was talking to him up there,' and promptly departed.

It is so easy to forget that prayer is all about a relationship with God. We are not earning points for artistic expression or theological content in the prayers which we execute. We are simply talking to our Father in ordinary ways about ordinary situations. I for my part had to recognize my fault, share it with Katey (not so very easy but a good reason for establishing the ground explained above) and do something about it. In this way I managed to battle through my criticism and Katey hers.

Katey found my need to 'preach' at her very irritating, especially the tone of voice I would employ and my tendency to use any new theological term I had discovered at every possible opportunity. This all had to be talked through and dealt with. However, we still get a good laugh from my 'preaching' voice.

Finally under this heading I can point out that falling asleep while praying is not a sin. It first happened to me at what is called, in shorthand, an O.I.C.C.U. D.P.M. which roughly translated means the Oxford Inter-Collegiate Christian Union Daily Prayer Meeting! I was eagerly looking forward to participating but found that the cumulative effect of the late night rigours of finishing an essay, the easy-chair into which I had slumped and the warmth within the room was one of sleep rather than spiritual warfare. I could only have dropped off for a few moments, but I awoke with a start as my head dropped and immediately pretended that I had been deeply engrossed in prayer. I was acutely embarrassed. Nobody said anything fortunately and I left feeling how dreadfully unspiritual I had been.

Katey and I have nodded off in the middle of praying together. We are no longer embarrassed (the party who fell asleep) nor critical (the party who stayed awake) but just take it in our stride. We see it as the practical outworking of 'snoring in the Spirit'!

4. Dare to be different

If there is one thing that blunts our prayer life it's repetition. We both need to agree to take responsibility to stop our prayer time from getting locked into a set system or form. Here are a few ways to prevent this from happening.

Initiation is important. Introduce a new element into your prayer life. Share a thought that strikes you following your partner's prayer (we will look at this in more detail when we consider the gifts of the Spirit). A preparedness to initiate within the framework of our prayer life will keep the whole relationship fresh and act as a safeguard against creating that 'holy silence' that brooks no interruption.

Indeed, interruption is another important element. We must not be ruled by our time of prayer but rather utilize it practically and effectively. After the style of a well-known scripture, prayer was designed for man and not man for prayer. We often interrupt our time of prayer to offer to pray for the other. This is altogether better than suddenly rising, gliding across the room, clamping hands on your partner and praying. All you need is a few words such as, 'I'd like to pray for you about . . .' and then whatever the issue is. Normality and clarity are important ingredients in our prayer life.

▶ *Action stations*

For this you will need a Bible, pen and paper each, and thirty minutes to sit down together. Don't panic; this is not thirty minutes of prayer but an opportunity to look at and learn from what the Bible has to say about prayer.

Agree how you will tackle the passages. Will one of you look them up and read them? Will you take it in turns? Who will keep their finger in the book and guide the discussion forward? Settle these practical questions.

Having done so, pray together using the Lord's prayer. Now work your way through the scriptures, discussing your own thoughts and noting your conclusions as you go.

Prayer the precursor

A precursor means that which runs before, something which precedes. A quick look at Scripture confirms that prayer always precedes the activity of God.

When Jesus faced the task of choosing twelve close friends to learn from him, he disappeared to pray first (Lk 6:12 ff.). He went out into the hills and spent the whole night praying to God. When morning came he called the disciples to him and chose twelve of them whom he designated apostles. Jesus talked to his Father to discover whom he should gather around him. He wanted to co-operate with God. It was essential that he selected the right people in whom to invest his life (and not simply his knowledge). These folk would be the pioneers of the New Testament church and the Christian message.

Again, we see the place of prayer preceding revelation. Jesus praying in private together with his disciples breaks off to pose a question, 'Who do the crowds say I am?' (Lk 9:18). A number of answers are given, all wide of the mark, when Jesus homes in on the disciples and develops his question by saying, 'Who do you say I am?' (Lk 9:20). This obviously increases the stakes somewhat; no one wants to open their mouth only to put their foot in it. However, before he can check himself Peter blurts out, 'You are the Messiah, the Son of the living God' (Mt 16:16). Jesus does not congratulate him as such, but indicates that that which Peter has expressed was not discerned by any human analysis or computation but had been revealed directly from God. Peter had had a unique revelation; God had spoken directly to him and used him to communicate the unique truth about Jesus.

About a week later this revelation was followed by another entrusted to Peter, John and James. While praying Jesus was transfigured and the three disciples, on the verge of falling asleep, were suddenly totally awake as a piece of high drama took place before their eyes. Bold Peter again opened his mouth but this time let slip a somewhat inappropriate comment. The disciples kept this revelation to themselves, not quite appreciating its meaning at the time.

Briefly looking at Acts chapter 2 we see the disciples were together, no doubt praying for God to do something having convinced them to stay in Jerusalem, probably the most unhealthy spot for any follower of Jesus at that time. The 'something' of God was the outpouring of the Holy Spirit, the person of the Godhead who provided those who had seen the risen Lord with the confidence and power to proclaim as much within a hostile environment.

A little later in Acts 2:42 we find the early church devoting itself to prayer, i.e. seeking to beat in time with the heart of God so that the work of God might flourish, and being ready to take an active part in that.

▶ Remember

Prayer always precedes the activity of God. If you do not see much of God's activity around you, pray honestly and stand back, for God will act. We need to be people who hear from God direct; we desperately require unique first-hand revelation. I find it rather sad that so often as I travel I find Christians informing me that what the latest 'big name' preacher has declared is currently the heart of God. I have nothing against what they have preached; my concern is that Christians are getting their revelations second-hand. Many are enjoying God vicariously, i.e. through the experience of another, rather than meeting God face to face themselves.

Take a look at 1 John 2:27—'As for you, Christ has poured out his Spirit on you. As long as his Spirit remains in you, you do not need anyone to teach you. For his Spirit teaches you about everything and what he teaches is true not false. Obey the Spirit's teaching, then, and remain in union with Christ.' God wants to speak to us directly, and we have the capacity to communicate with him one to one, for he has given us his Holy Spirit to enable us to have 'face-to-face' discussion. I believe every one of us should discover what it is to talk with God directly and enjoy personal and unique revelation. As a couple you can do this together; as you get practice in this so your confidence and competence will grow.

Submit to God not to circumstance

In Luke 22:39-46 we read the heart-rending story of Jesus in the Garden of Gethsemane. As he agonized in prayer with his Father he was confronted with the way of suffering which lay ahead and every part of his humanity recoiled and drew back. However, having poured out his heart with all the emotion and anguish that he felt, even to the extent of sweating drops of blood, Jesus agreed to obey God and serve his eternal and divine will. Jesus had expressed himself in total honesty before God. There was nothing super-spiritual about his agreeing to go to the cross; he didn't gloss over the pain and the anguish he felt but ultimately determined to place his hand in God's hand and to hang on tight.

For many Christians calamity or difficult circumstances direct them away from God. They become so full of the pain and pressure of their circumstances that God gets crowded out and the relationship falls into disrepair. Some even choose to reject God himself as the very source of the problem and direct their anger and bitterness against him. It is very sad when we allow ourselves to be robbed of a close and loving relationship with God through the nature of our circumstances. When times are tough that should be the moment to close ranks with our heavenly Father. In the face of disaster we should find ourselves driven into the arms of love waiting to encircle us.

When Katey and I discovered that we had a less than 1% chance of having a baby we found that we were driven into each other's arms. We needed each other; we needed affection and acceptance like there was no tomorrow. We also discovered how much we needed God, and held tightly in his arms we could express the anger, pour out the anguish and sob quietly into his chest as he held us close in arms of unimaginable love and security. We also discovered that instead of being crushed beneath the weight of the problem we were able to develop a godly perspective on it and develop a sufficient sense of proportion to continue functioning in everyday life.

As couples we will find a greater capacity to ride through life when we choose to do so within the arms of God. We need to get used to resting in his embrace and experiencing his love so that we know to whom we can turn if and when circumstances swing against us. Practice getting into God's presence and gaining a godly perspective.

Perseverance

Luke 18:1 informs us to pray and not to give up—and this is sound advice. Muller, who did so much for children in need within his own day and age, prayed regularly for four friends that they might become Christians. During his lifetime he saw three of those friends enter into a relationship with God. However, the fourth one resisted and it was not until after Muller had died that he found the faith Muller had consistently prayed that he would find.

There is much to be said for maintaining prayer for specific situations and not giving up on them. So often we give up partly because we lose heart and partly because we lose originality in approaching the object of our prayer and so become bored. A little thought can ensure that you remain constant in prayer and find new ways to pray for the situation.

For example, when we were praying for one couple over a number of years we began spending time thinking about them and their situation, and although our object was that they should discover the reality of Christian

71

experience for themselves we seldom prayed to that specific end. We began to pray for their circumstances—certain friendships, pressures etc—and all sorts of other obstacles that impeded their perceiving Jesus for who he was and how he related to them and vice versa. This became creative and enjoyable; our faith for them increased and we were able to persevere prayerfully. So remember, if at first you don't see answers—persevere!

5
Worship

The heart of worship

In the early stages of our married life there was one question which consistently stumped me—that question was: 'Mike, do you love me?' Now if I said yes it sounded dismissive and perfunctory, yet if I tried to establish the fact that I did love Katey it sounded rather strained, listing all the ways by which my wife could realize she was loved. In the film *Fiddler on the Roof* Tevye asks his wife whether she loves him. Her response, in song, is to identify all she does for him: 'I cook for you, I wash for you, I clean for you,' all of which is a long way from reassuring Tevye that he is loved.

I'm still faced with the same question today, eight years further on in my married life, and I've learned just how important it is to express frequently and verbally that I love Katey. It is important for Katey to tell me of her love as well. Strange though it might seem, one never grows tired of that little word 'love', and as we express it with our lips we will often demonstrate its reality with a hug, kiss or some similar act of affection.

Sadly, where love is not spoken, the demonstration in the physical realm also falls into disrepair. Remember all we said earlier about the importance of communication.

God longs for a deep and vibrant relationship with people. Having wooed a rebellious people throughout history he ultimately made the final play for their affection and obedience by commissioning his own Son to reinstate a relationship between himself and man that was in a state of extreme disrepair. I can imagine that momentous occasion in heaven when with something of a heavy heart the Father approached his Son and entered into conversation with him. 'Son,' he said.

'Yes, Father,' came Jesus' eager reply.

'Son, I've a task to undertake in which I need your full co-operation. Will you help me?'

'You know I will, Father, it will be a privilege.'

'But wait, let me explain. You know when at the beginning of time we had such fun creating the heaven and the earth and everything on the earth, and how as a finale to all that we created man in our image?'

'Yes, I remember. Marvellous fun!'

'And you remember how having been created as a companion man chose to rebel against us, do his own thing and break faith with us. And how we had to banish him from all this.' God waved his arm in an expansive circle indicating all that the eye could see round about them. 'We lost that friendship we'd enjoyed with him. Well, Son, the time has come to renew that friendship.'

'Father, that's tremendous. I'm thrilled you want me involved.'

'Wait till I've spoken further. I need you to lay aside your royal prerogative and privilege and allow yourself to become a man. To leave this place and live on earth, showing mankind what God is like and living as man was always meant to live.'

'I can do that.'

'Yes, but the men among whom you live will misunderstand your message. They'll begin to hate you. They'll despise and reject you, and even your friends will desert you and leave you alone.'

'Father, hard though that is I would want to do it if it pleases you.'

'Well, these same people will falsely accuse you, they will arrest and abuse you and finally kill you by nailing you to a wooden gibbet in the same way they would rid themselves of a common criminal.'

'That is hard to contemplate, but if it will restore our relationship with man I will go.'

'That's not the worst of it, Son.' And tears began to well up in the eyes of the Almighty as he continued. 'While your battered body hangs suspended on that gibbet I will gather up all the sin and corruption of sin-sick society from its beginning through its present right up to its end and hurl it at you. For the first time in all eternity I will break fellowship with you for I cannot bear to look on sin. Though you cry out to me I shall not answer until the deed is done, sin is dealt with and friendship with man once more a possibility.'

I believe that in the silence that followed, both Father and Son sensed the pain and the cost involved. As we know, Jesus agreed to obey his Father and fulfilled that marvellous unfathomable work of salvation for all mankind. It is in this activity of God that we understand the nature and meaning of love. 'Dear friends, let us love one another, because love comes from God. Whoever loves is a child of God and knows God. Whoever does not love does not know God, for God is love' (1 Jn 4:7-8). Even more remarkable, it was not the lovely but the unlovely that God died for. Mankind was not eagerly demanding a saviour like Jesus, but quite content serving his own interests. Yet love could see beyond this and took action.

What I am constantly thrilled by is the way in which love initiates. God initiated reconciliation and restoration, and so in our marriages the onus is always upon us to take the initiative in reconciliation. In this way, we express our faith in a most practical way. We also renew and refresh our marriage. It may mean swallowing our pride and becoming vulnerable. This is the cost of Christian marriage. Katey and I have learned that the best thing about a bust-up is the getting it back together again. The apology and the renewal of our relationship. Acknowledging and laying aside the wrong in order to give oneself 110% to one's partner again. I for one always find it very hard to say sorry, even when I know I'm wrong and have accepted as much. However, it is the very action that brings about the reconciliation. And this lies at the heart of our worship life together.

The reality of worship

Let's look at Romans 12:1-2. Paul writes,

> So then, my brothers, because of God's great mercy to us [which I've just outlined above], I appeal to you: Offer yourselves as a living sacrifice to God, dedicated to his service and pleasing to him. Do not conform yourselves to the standards of this world, but let God transform you inwardly by a complete change of your mind. Then you will be able to know the will of God—what is good and is pleasing to him and is perfect.

Here is expressed the very nature of true worship— total availability to God. Notice that this condition is reached by the renewal and not by the removal of your mind. We are called to be involved in this process at every level. This text is as appropriate to relating together in marriage as it is in relating to our heavenly Father.

How does worship feature in our marriage? Well, I for one worship Katey and she worships me. I worship her verbally—I tell her I love her, I think she's fantastic, she does me good, I want to do her good, she's the only girl for me. I worship her physically—I kiss her, cuddle her, hold hands with her, make love to her. I think she is worth all of my attention and invite her to make whatever demands she might want to. I am totally available to her—there is no area of my life from which I wish to exclude her, and she has freedom to address me on any issue.

This aspect of worship in marriage is highlighted in the biblical charge to married couples to leave, cleave and become one flesh. The word 'cleave' literally means 'to hold fast to one another' as on a 'glutinous surface'. That's precisely what we must do, both in our marital relationship and in our relationship with God.

When we turn to looking at our worship of God, Paul actually calls us to abandon ourselves to the goodness of God. So often we hold back on giving all to God when he has bought us lock, stock and barrel. He expects us to be totally available to him. Unfortunately, however, because of culture—it's not our custom to leap about; or tradition—we are uncomfortable without someone directing us; or peer group pressure—what will my friends think if I put my hands in the air or if I don't put my hands in the air, we respond to a myriad different voices none of which is God's. We are called to respond to him alone, regardless of the consequences. Indeed, if you are obedient to God the consequences cannot be damaging in the long term.

I well remember when God put me through my paces in this. I was not at all sure about dancing in worship and believed I would feel exceptionally uncomfortable if I did leap around during a time of praise. Although I sensed that God wanted me to dance, my own self-consciousness held me back. However, I was bullied into it through the godly perseverance of Ishmael, one Spring Harvest, and found I did not feel foolish, my inhibitions went and a new sense of liberty and love in my relationship with God was released. This is not to say that everyone should follow suit. This was God's word and way for me. It might be for you too, but you'll know if it is because God makes himself abundantly plain.

A second incident developed from this in that God convicted me about my bad moods. I would walk around at home looking like a thunder-cloud and generating an unhealthy atmosphere. The tragedy of this was not only that I distanced myself from God but also from Katey. She couldn't get close to me even if she wanted to, and didn't know how to approach me without setting off a thermonuclear explosion!

One day God highlighted a verse from the Bible to me—not an especially frequent occurrence. It was 1 Thessalonians 5:16-18: 'Be joyful always, pray at all times, be thankful in all circumstances. This is what God wants from you in your life union with Christ Jesus.' I was not feeling much like praising or giving thanks, and was a little irritated by the way God nudged me and said, 'That's for you and I want you to put it into practice.' I, of course, entered into a long debate with God as to why I couldn't and wouldn't. But he had other plans.

Ecclesiastes 4:12 contains the immortal words: 'A rope made of three cords is hard to break.' It was a verse used at our wedding and roughly translated means that in a Christian marriage there is a partnership of three—the husband, the wife and the Lord. This means, of course, that there is the possibility of a majority decision to resolve any dispute. A husband and wife who choose to neglect God's ways can form an unholy alliance and vote God out of every decision. They are the poorer, but it happens. However, there is also the possibility of the husband or wife teaming up with God to outvote the rebellion and intransigence of the other partner. This is what happened to me.

Somehow Katey discovered what God had said to me about giving thanks in all circumstances. This spelt disaster—there is nothing worse than when your partner agrees you are wrong and you know you are too and are going to have to give in. What happened from the moment the Holy Spirit split on me to Katey was that I would stomp around the kitchen in a foul mood. Katey, in an endearing way, would stop what she was doing and say, 'You know what you've got to do, don't you?' And I would think, 'And you know what you can do, don't you?' but say, 'Yes.' Not content with making me feel uncomfortable she would go on to bully me into praising God! So with a voice empty of emotion and with a touch of cynicism I would say, 'Praise the Lord! Hallelujah! Glory!' By this time Katey had had enough (and God too I guess) and she would give me some VBH (verbal bodily harm), put on a worship cassette and bully me into worshipping.

The most galling thing of all—it worked. Slowly I began to apologize to God and Katey, and started praising God, worshipping him, telling him how marvellous he was, how I was completely his and how I wanted to turn to him in praise and thanksgiving at the first hint of a mood. Best of all, neither God nor Katey exploited their victory but just joined in and we had a smashing time.

We must learn that it is through our worship that we will be conformed to Christ. In a world which seeks to overwhelm us and form us in its image, we need to turn our lives wholly over to God which is true worship. As we serve him and promote his ways then we enable people to see Jesus in us—we become God's highway through a crippled world. C. S. Lewis said that Christians are 'little Christs', and as we abandon ourselves to Jesus we become his effective hands and feet in a world in which people are reaching out to touch him.

Worship, therefore, must form a significant part of our prayer life together as couples. We often pray but do not worship together. The prayerful expression of our worship of God is the love and praise of our hearts expressed with our lips. So infrequently do we really take time to praise God that few people can wax eloquent about the goodness, grace and loveliness of God. When we begin to worship God verbally, concentrating on his love and acknowledging our submission to him, we are released from the self-preoccupation that prevents us from serving our partner and God himself.

We so often seek after God for our own obvious benefit, to get from him rather than to give to him. So often the Sunday worship service is filled with folk all trying to take something from God for their own tattered lives rather than ministering their love to God that he might minister to someone else's tattered life. It seems all wrong that as we gather together Sunday by Sunday we all hope that God will meet our individual needs. Surely we come together to celebrate God, to proclaim that he is alive and full of loving care for us.

We each have testimony to God's goodness during the preceding week. From our fellowship with him and with others within the body, we should come overflowing with praise for him, ready to heap honour upon his name and literally lift the roof with our declaration of his worth. Obviously, there will be the wounded among us. We ourselves may need first-aid, perhaps even major surgery, but we will be all the more able to receive this when we stand among a group of people whose focus is Jesus, whose lives are sold out to Jesus, whose hearts are full of Jesus and hence whose ministry is to bring us Jesus.

Katey and I soon discovered that worship needed to be a key part of our prayer life together. We needed to abandon ourselves to God constantly. We had to recognize that the fruit of self-preoccupation was to become problem centred, and that meant the very life of Jesus was squeezed out of us like juice from a lemon. What was more, we very quickly caught self-preoccupation off one another and so both of us got squeezed dry. This led us away from the Lord, produced friction in our relationship and gave good ground for Satan to stamp all over. We had to practise challenging one another with the goodness and grace and loveliness of Jesus.

In one period of our married life we were skint beyond all skintness. After our outgoings we had the princely sum of £4 per week available for housekeeping. Katey was not at all impressed when I pressed four crisp one-pound notes into her hand at the beginning of the week and told her to bring me the change. Needless to say, we were well provided for by the Lord. However, we did find that the financial situation placed great pressure upon us. It was easy to dwell on it, to grow self-preoccupied and full of envy for everyone else's lifestyle. You only realize what a difference the occasional little treat makes when you can't afford any.

Often, feeling somewhat crushed, we discovered what a release it was to recognize that we belonged to God and that he loved us. Rather like David in some of his psalms, we'd stare at each other confronted by our 'raw deal', focus on Jesus and finish up absolutely amazed by his love. Of course, this didn't always work. We failed, got furious, ranted and raved, but we were able to extract a priceless principle and practise it on several occasions. Indeed, as time passed we got better and better at applying the principle.

If we apply the principle of worship in all circumstances we will fill our Sunday worship with the fragrance of Jesus. Often when we gather together we are empty of things to declare. We have nothing to offer Jesus because we have an impoverished personal experience. In our corporate gatherings we are often challenged and motivated to pray or seek God, only to find that we can never get it together in our personal experience simply because there are no foundations upon which to build. Hence this manual. With an effective and active personal life of devotion we can all gather together with every expectation that each will bring a psalm, hymn or spiritual song (Eph 5:19)—and fresh ones, not ones we have contributed dutifully every week for as long as anyone can remember!

Worship brings us into the presence of God. We can simply enjoy God for who he is. It is essential in enabling us to grow in confidence in the character of God, so that when we run into a time of pressure or difficulty we can fully trust the God who is with us in it. We need to take time to develop that confidence, for it takes time for our intellectual knowledge of God to become established as an experiential knowledge of God. So often when we meet an adversity we have an insufficient reservoir of experiential knowledge of God to give us the confidence within the situation.

When we began to face the reality of childlessness it was hard to do anything more than give grudging assent to the compassion and goodness of God. However, as we have worshipped God regularly it has become easier to entrust him with the situation, knowing he has everything fully under control, he's rooting for us and that he is full of goodness towards us. There is a lightness within us now in this whole area which has proved most creative.

We do not believe that as Christians we can steer a successful course through life unless we are absolutely convinced of the character of God. In these days when it is fashionable to add a qualification to every statement of absolute truth we all too easily find ourselves stepping back from the absolute faithfulness and goodness of God, his omnipotence and omniscience and every other aspect of his character. You cannot have a God whose character is in need of qualification. Either God is God or not God at all. We must accept the absolutes of his character and live in practical recognition of them.

We are a people of certainties in an uncertain world. We are a body of stability when life itself appears to be disintegrating around us. We worship a God who is eternal and whose character remains unchanging through the bleakest of experiences. We find ourselves secure in the palm of his hand as the dust of disturbance which has struck our life settles and we regain a sense of perspective. Our God reigns, and we reign with him. As A.W. Tozer points out in *The Knowledge of the Holy,*

> The most portentous fact about any man is not what he at a given moment may say or do, but what he in his deep heart conceives God to be like . . . The essence of idolatry is the entertainment of thoughts about God that are unworthy of him . . . . The idolator simply imagines things about God and acts as if they were true.

We must at all times beware of idolatry. By active worship, releasing ourselves completely to God, we can both comprehend and develop a complete assurance in his character.

Worship keeps us rooted in God. As Jim Wallis points out in *The Call to Conversion*, 'What roots are to a tree, worship is to the Christian.' We need to retain those roots to draw from the water of life, so sustaining our life and enabling further growth and maturity.

Let's be practical

Having said all this about worship, what is our way forward together? Well, as Katey and I realized the need to take time to focus on God alone we found we shared the same practical problems. Neither of us was musical—I sang somewhat flat, and we both felt embarrassed even at the thought of singing or dancing in worshipful abandon in front of each other. Strange really since we are quite at ease and fairly extrovert in any social gathering of friends. As with everything else in this area of praying together, we had to agree simply to get on with it and see what happened.

When we got together to pray we decided to play a game! One of us would say a word which described one aspect of God's character such as 'grace'. The other would then have to respond by speaking out the first word that came into their head. This was fun, fast and furious. It also pushed any embarrassment to the back of our mind and introduced a very positive element of humour. Any pauses and the culprit would have to sing a chorus which got us launched into singing together without the need of instruments.

Furthermore, sometimes the word one of us spoke out revealed that we had a blind spot or certain reservations about the trustworthy nature of God's character, and so we were able to talk these through together. Sometimes a word might cause us to pause and talk about its particular reference to both God and ourselves. An example might run: grace, goodness, kindness, faithfulness, mercy, justice, love, pain. At which point we would stop to look at pain with reference to ourselves and to God, to reaffirm that in spite of pain God was knowable in the midst of pain. We discovered that biblical references came to mind, for example 2 Corinthians 1:3-5 speaking of the comfort of Christ overflowing in the midst of lives that experience the sufferings of Christ. We would talk about the verse, exchange ideas and maybe meditate upon it before moving on to bombard the gates of heaven with prayers of praise to which our meditation had given birth.

As we became comfortable with this we discovered that one of us did have the courage, if not always the voice, to start up a worship song. Together we would sing and get excited in God. Indeed for a while our whole time of prayer together consisted of worshipping and praising God. It was terrific and provided the source of much practical blessing from the person of God himself.

Having gained a little confidence Katey retrieved her recorder from the loft and bullied me into blowing the cobwebs off my guitar—a memento from the days when as a teenager I had struggled to master classical skills on this instrument—and together we would just play away making music which surprisingly enough was often quite tuneful. The next step on from here was to add lyrics of our own. These were usually spontaneous and forgotten the instant they had been uttered, but they often brought us both very close to the person of Jesus and ministered to us most effectively. The further we progressed the less inhibited we became and the more willing to contribute to larger meetings in which we were involved. We also discovered we had a rich reservoir of God-centred experience to share from, and the more we contributed publicly the less self-conscious we became and the more aware of the Spirit of God. God was blessed, we were encouraged and the body was built up. How very biblical!

We have all been formed in the image of God, and God is a creator. The creative quality of God is in every one of us. Many of us never have the opportunity to express that creativity. Our artistic efforts as children may have been scorned, so we have never developed this area. Yet we can all be creative. In our working together we can experiment with our creativity. We can stimulate and encourage each other. This is both a positive experience and tremendous fun.

▶ Action stations

Hopefully you are both excited by all that we have written above. We suggest you set aside half an hour together for a bit of worshipful fun. Be prepared to enjoy yourselves. Why not start by having a romantic meal together first and then, fully relaxed, take time for the activities that follow. You will need a Bible handy and maybe a song book.

We mentioned above how we got involved in worship by playing the word game. This is the place where you too can start.

Firstly, read aloud Colossians 1:15-23:

> Christ is the visible likeness of the invisible God. He is the first-born Son, superior to all created things. For through him God created everything in heaven and on earth, the seen and the unseen things, including spiritual powers, lords, rulers, and authorities. God created the whole universe through him and for him. Christ existed before all things, and in union with him all things have their proper place. He is the head of his body, the church; he is the first-

86

born Son, who was raised from the dead, in order that he alone might have the first place in all things. For it was by God's own decision that the Son has in himself the full nature of God. Through the Son, then, God decided to bring the whole universe back to himself. God made peace through his Son's death on the cross and so brought back to himself all things, both on earth and in heaven. At one time you were far away from God and were his enemies because of the evil things you did and thought. But now, by means of the physical death of his Son, God has made you his friends, in order to bring you, holy, pure, and faultless, into his presence. You must, of course, continue faithful on a firm and sure foundation, and must not allow yourselves to be shaken from the hope you gained when you heard the gospel. It is of this gospel that I, Paul, became a servant—this gospel which has been preached to everybody in the world.

Now, thinking about the uniqueness of Jesus Christ, one after the other, and quite rapidly, speak out words or short phrases which spring to mind following your partner's declaration. Wives could start with the words, 'Jesus is supreme,' and then the men respond.

If and when you dry up, break and ask each other the following question in turn: 'What particularly struck a chord with you during that word sequence?' You may remember a scripture, so read it and talk about it. An incident may have been recalled—describe it and chat over why it was recalled. All the time relate back to God.

Having done this, play the word game again, only this time use something from your previous discussion to instigate it—and why not sing a chorus if you are guilty of hesitation?

To end this time of activity, stand up, hold hands and sing the chorus 'I just want to praise you' or another one you know.

In closing may we suggest that if you are musical you

worship God together utilizing your musical skills. Gather the Sunday magazines together and produce a worship collage. You could even adorn your living-room wall with it and it could become a unique talking-point. If you have literary gifts why not contribute a poem to your worship? In all these ways we can discover the reality of the character and personality of Father God and release the love in our hearts to him.

We have discovered the activity outlined above to be one of our most fruitful experiences together, and we know you will too. Let us know how you get on. (You can write to us c/o the publishers of this book, Kingsway Publications.)

6

Discovering the Gifts of the Holy Spirit

It seems that the slightest mention of the Holy Spirit can cause blood pressure to rise, tension to creep in and attitudes to harden. This is very sad since the Holy Spirit is the person of the Godhead who remains here in our world to convict the pagan of guilt and righteousness and to assure the Christian of salvation.

I remember a friend informing me of a particularly sad story he had read in a Sunday supplement. It concerned Percy the Penguin. Percy had been born at a zoo but his mother had taken one look at him and instantly quit motherhood. Poor Percy was now an orphan. However, that gallant band of men we know as zookeepers adopted baby Percy and bottle fed him, ensuring he passed through those critical early weeks and months. The day eventually came for Percy to be returned to the penguin pool to live among his own kind as, naturally enough, a penguin.

The zookeepers gathered around the edge of the enclosure as Percy was introduced to his cousins and they all seemed to get on very well. Greetings over they all filed towards the pool and dived in one after the other—

except that is for Percy. He dutifully shuffled along in the awkward yet orderly line of penguins, but when he reached the edge of the pool he held back and just stared at the water below. Obviously assuming that Percy was overcome at his first sight of water, one of the friendly keepers approached from behind and gave Percy a helpful push into the pool. No sooner had Percy hit the water than he flew like an arrow back onto the side of the pool. He gave the guilty keeper something of an accusing look and would no doubt have accompanied this with a bit of beak had he not been brought up in the best of circles.

A little concerned, the keepers had a brief discussion before advancing on Percy as a body and tipping him back into the pool. Percy once again shot back onto the side. No matter how hard they tried to convince him to swim, Percy was having none of it. The article concluded that Percy was the only penguin in the zoo who detested water.

Amusing though such a story appears, it is sad because Percy had been designed for water. Anyone who has seen a penguin waddling across terra firma recognizes that they are not the most elegant or adept land-based animal. However, place them in water and they twist and turn and perform all kinds of aquabatics revealing that this is the environment for which they were surely designed. Percy, equipped in every way and to a high degree of proficiency for an aqueous environment, refused to experience the life for which he had been designed.

You and I have been designed as containers for the Holy Spirit—God's gift of himself to each and every one of us. Having been born of the Spirit we are to live in the Spirit and keep in step with the Spirit (Gal 5:25). Since the Holy Spirit, despatched by none other than Jesus himself, is the person of the Godhead who takes up residence in the life of the individual Christian, it is little wonder that he is vital to the work of communicating with the Godhead. And since prayer is all about communication, we all need to know, appreciate and cooperate with him.

For many of us our prayer lives have been barren of reality for no other reason than that we have misunderstood, neglected or denigrated the person and work of the Holy Spirit. Now is the time to take a look at who he is and what his work is. Then we will see where this fits into our prayer life together.

▶ *Action stations*

You will need Bibles, and pencil and paper if you wish to make notes. One of you look up the references, the other read the verses and then together answer the questions. Before we go any further, however, note four very important points:

(1) The Holy Spirit is a him not an it. Look up John 16:7-8 for one reference to this fact.

(2) He always points us to Jesus (Jn 16:14).

(3) He is for every believer—there are no first-class/second-class divides in the Christian family. Peter points out the promise of the Spirit is for all (Acts 2:38-39).

(4) Finally, in Scripture his coming was usually accompanied by evidence of spiritual gifts. Turn on a few pages to Acts 10:46.

Having established those four points we want you now to look together at several encounters with the Holy Spirit. The encounter of Jesus, the disciples, the early church and finally ourselves. Do set aside a useful period of time, say twenty minutes, for this and make whatever notes you feel might prove helpful to refer to later. If you have not got a Bible handy the verses are quoted in full for your use.

1. *Jesus encounters the Holy Spirit*

After all the people had been baptized, Jesus also was baptized. While he was praying, heaven was opened, and the Holy Spirit came down on him in bodily form like a dove. And a voice came from heaven, 'You are my own dear Son. I am pleased with you.' When Jesus began his work, he was about thirty years old (Lk 3:21-23).

Jesus returned from the Jordan full of the Holy Spirit and was led by the Spirit into the desert, where he was tempted by the Devil for forty days. In all that time he ate nothing, so that he was hungry when it was over.

The Devil said to him, 'If you are God's Son, order this stone to turn into bread.'

But Jesus answered, 'The scripture says, "Man cannot live on bread alone."'

Then the Devil took him up and showed him in a second all the kingdoms of the world. 'I will give you all this power and all this wealth,' the Devil told him. 'It has all been handed over to me, and I can give it to anyone I choose. All this will be yours, then, if you worship me.'

Jesus answered, 'The scripture says, "Worship the Lord your God and serve only him!"'

Then the Devil took him to Jerusalem and set him on the highest point of the Temple, and said to him, 'If you are God's Son, throw yourself down from here. For the scripture says, "God will order his angels to take good care of you." It also says, "They will hold you up with their hands so that not even your feet will be hurt on the stones."'

But Jesus answered, 'The scripture says, "Do not put the Lord your God to the test."'

When the Devil finished tempting Jesus in every way, he

left him for a while.

Then Jesus returned to Galilee, and the power of the Holy Spirit was with him. The news about him spread throughout all that territory. He taught in the synagogues and was praised by everyone (Lk 4:1-15).

a) Describe from the passage what happened when Jesus was baptized.
b) Who was it that led Jesus into the desert?
c) How is Jesus described on his return from the Jordan?
d) How is Jesus described on his return to Galilee?

2. *The disciples encounter the Holy Spirit*

When the day of Pentecost came, all the believers were gathered together in one place. Suddenly there was a noise from the sky which sounded like a strong wind blowing, and it filled the whole house where they were sitting. Then they saw what looked like tongues of fire which spread out and touched each person there. They were all filled with the Holy Spirit and began to talk in other languages, as the Spirit enabled them to speak.

There were Jews living in Jerusalem, religious men who had come from every country in the world. When they heard this noise, a large crowd gathered. They were all excited, because each one of them heard the believers speaking in his own language. In amazement and wonder they exclaimed, 'These people who are talking like this are Galileans! How is it, then, that all of us hear them speaking in our own native languages? We are from Parthia, Media, and Elam; from Mesopotamia, Judaea, and Cappadocia; from Pontus and Asia, from Phrygia and Pamphylia, from Egypt and the regions of Libya near Cyrene. Some of us are from Rome, both Jews and Gentiles converted to Judaism, and some of us are from Crete and Arabia—yet all of us hear them speaking in our own languages about the great things that God has done!' Amazed and confused, they kept asking each other, 'What does this mean?'

But others made fun of the believers, saying, 'These people are drunk!' (Acts 2:1-13).

a) What was the day on which the disciples were filled with the Spirit?

b) Where were the disciples?

c) What happened when they were filled with the Holy Spirit?

d) What was the reaction of various groups within the crowd?

3. *The early church encounters the Holy Spirit*

So Ananias went, entered the house where Saul was, and placed his hands on him. 'Brother Saul,' he said, 'the Lord has sent me—Jesus himself, who appeared to you on the road as you were coming here. He sent me so that you might see again and be filled with the Holy Spirit.' At once something like fish scales fell from Saul's eyes, and he was able to see again. He stood up and was baptized; and after he had eaten, his strength came back (Acts 9:17-19).

While Apollos was in Corinth, Paul travelled through the interior of the province and arrived in Ephesus. There he found some disciples and asked them, 'Did you receive the Holy Spirit when you became believers?'

'We have not heard that there is a Holy Spirit,' they answered.

'Well, then, what kind of baptism did you receive?' Paul asked.

'The baptism of John,' they answered.

Paul said, 'The baptism of John was for those who turned from their sins; and he told the people of Israel to believe in the one who was coming after him—that is, in Jesus.'

When they heard this, they were baptized in the name of the Lord Jesus.

Paul placed his hands on them, and the Holy Spirit came upon them; they spoke in strange tongues and also proclaimed God's message. They were about twelve men in all (Acts 19:1-7).

a) What did Ananias do and what did he pray when he was with Saul?

b) What happened when Saul was filled with the Holy Spirit?

c) What baptism had the disciples at Ephesus received?

d) What happened when the Ephesian disciples were filled with the Holy Spirit?

4. *Are we to encounter the Holy Spirit?*

I have told you this while I am still with you. The Helper, the Holy Spirit, whom the Father will send in my name, will teach you everything and make you remember all that I have told you.

Peace is what I leave with you; it is my own peace that I give you. I do not give it as the world does. Do not be worried and upset; do not be afraid (Lk 14:25-27).

But when the Holy Spirit comes upon you, you will be filled with power, and you will be witnesses for me in Jerusalem, in all Judaea and Samaria, and to the ends of the earth (Acts 1:8).

a) What does Jesus promise us when the Holy Spirit comes upon us?

b) What is that power for?

c) What names does Jesus give the Holy Spirit?

d) What two things does Jesus tell us to be?

It should be evident from your Scripture research that the Christian is designed to be a container for the Holy Spirit. It is he who gives us the power to live as Christians and provides the vital communication link with Father God. It is essential that we are filled with the Holy Spirit at every moment of every day. Ephesians 5:18 commands us to 'be filled with the Spirit'. The tense is the present continuous, so the actual meaning is 'go on being filled with the Holy Spirit'. We all need to be full to overflowing with the Holy Spirit if we are to prove effective disciples. Furthermore, communication is two way and God guides us and provides us with privileged information by means of the Holy Spirit. This is so valuable, especially when praying for people and situations.

If you feel powerless or distant from God, pause and take a moment now to invite your partner to pray that you might be filled with the Holy Spirit. There's no need for special language or long prayers. Why not follow the pattern of Ananias and lay hands on your partner and pray simply for the Spirit's fullness. If while you are praying you sense you want to pray a particular prayer for your partner, do so and be a blessing to him or her. It's so lovely when we minister to one another in this way.

The fruit and the gifts of the Spirit

In Galatians 5:22 we read: 'But the Spirit produces love, joy, peace, patience, kindness, goodness, faithfulness, humility and self-control.' In one of our many moves we inherited a garden with a number of fruit trees in it. Being autumn we had no idea what kind of fruit they would bear. However, as the seasons passed and summer returned we were able to identify two apple trees and one pear tree. These trees could be trusted every year to produce apples or pears according to which type they were. We did not expect the apple tree to produce bananas one year, nor did we expect any of the trees to fail to produce.

As Christians the right fruit for our lives is outlined in the passage from Galatians quoted above. If the Holy Spirit is filling our lives then all this fruit should be evident. Where one or more are consistently absent we are in need of a little bit of tree surgery—the acts of the sinful nature need to be chopped off and room made for the Spirit of God to bring forth the crop for which we were originally designed. Since this is the natural fruit of the Christian's life then we do not have to struggle to enable it to flourish. If it is not flourishing then we must ask ourselves if we are filled with the Holy Spirit (if not, pray to be filled yourself or invite your partner to pray for you). If we are filled with the Spirit but still consistently fail to fruit in accordance with the gardener's description, then we need to give a little attention to those things which prevent successful fruiting and apply the correct pesticide. We will see how we do this in the very next chapter.

Scripture makes it very clear that the character of the Christian is marked by the fruit of the Spirit. Therefore if we take the name of Jesus to our lips there is no reason why our lives should not be marked by this fruit. If you are aware of weaknesses or a lack in your own or your partner's life make a note and be ready for 'Action Stations' at the end of this chapter.

God has not only given us the power to produce the fruit of the Spirit, giving our lives their distinctive Christian quality, but he has also empowered us with the gifts of the Spirit so that the church might be effectively serviced, individuals enabled to fruit in greater abundance and the world might be able to enjoy the effective communication of the reality of the love of God. Much has been written and spoken of concerning spiritual gifts, and there is usually a great deal of anticipation surrounding the subject. We have found the context of prayer in our marriage a very fruitful ground in which to discover, experiment with and experience the gifts of the Spirit.

If we turn to 1 Corinthians 12 we discover Paul's great desire that there should not be ignorance about spiritual gifts. We were ignorant of the Spirit for a number of years, let alone the gifts. I remember getting close to

turning from Christianity as a young disciple because of
my powerlessness and hypocrisy. I was involved in a very
active church and participating in evangelism, but while I
was smiling on the outside and communicating all the
promises of the gospel, I knew that inside I wasn't smiling; inside I wasn't experiencing the reality of those gospel promises. Now one thing I detest is hypocrisy. It was
this more than anything else that had turned me into an
ardent left-wing idealist when a teenager. I remember
walking the streets of Oxford talking to Katey and ex-
plaining to her that either Christianity was a deceit or
there was a conspiracy of silence about what made it
work effectively. Poor Katey, not long a Christian and
having to field all my reasoned doubts about the very
faith to which I had introduced her.

Getting towards the end of my tether and deciding to
make a clean break, we attended a talk one evening
about the Holy Spirit. We were both meeting different
groups of friends and so got separated at the meeting. It
wasn't until after the meeting that we met up again, both
waiting to speak to the preacher and discover more
about what he had said about the Holy Spirit and fullness. Having spoken to him he offered to pray, but only
after we had taken a walk on our own to decide if we
really wanted prayer.

As we walked I realized two things—first I felt a tremendous sense of excitement and anticipation, secondly
God seemed to be speaking directly and saying, 'My
power for your life in its entirety.' I wrestled for about
twenty minutes over the decision of whether to go
ahead. Although I had little conception of what giving
my life in its entirety meant, I knew that the issue was
serious and I would have to live with the consequences. I
finally decided to ask for prayer, and as the preacher laid
hands on me and prayed, after a few moments I saw

Jesus literally reach down and gather me in his arms and give me a wonderful embrace. I am not given to such moving experiences as a rule, but this was tremendous and I was lost in the presence of God, literally 'drunk in the Spirit' for quite a few minutes. For those who feel they have missed something, Katey, who was prayed for at the same time, felt absolutely nothing but just accepted that what you ask for you get (Lk 11:10) and thanked God for her new-found power to live for Jesus.

The gifts of the Spirit

It was not long after this time that we began to discover something of the gifts of the Spirit. When we had our first experience of speaking in tongues we decided it was time to consult the Bible to try and appreciate all that was going on. 1 Corinthians 12:8-10 lists the nine gifts of the Spirit. Paul was obviously comfortable with them, providing instructions for their right use to avoid their abuse which had been taking place within the Corinthian church. (Indeed, in the very first chapter of this letter, in verse 7, he encourages them by informing them that they do not lack any spiritual gift—and neither do we today.) However, our difficulty was that we were coming from a background which did not recognize the gifts of the Spirit, so we had to start from basics. We started by looking at the gifts one by one, and we will do the same now.

Wisdom

This gift is best illustrated by Solomon resolving the dispute between the two women both claiming maternal rights over the same baby (1 Kings 3:16-28). Not an easy task, but with divine wisdom Solomon brought the wrangle to a just and peaceful end. Further evidence of this gift is seen in the life of Jesus when he defused the potentially ugly scene that arose around the woman caught in adultery (Jn 8:1-11). It is evident to most involved in church life today that a mighty measure of this gift is required for the church to function as it should. Who's for wisdom?

Knowledge

When Jesus sat talking to the woman at the well (Jn 4), breaking every social convention and religious custom of the time, he had a clear word of knowledge about her marital situation. He knew she had no husband, that she had had five husbands and her current male companion was not her husband either. Something had been revealed to Jesus that he could not otherwise have known apart from the whisper of the Holy Spirit.

Katey had just such an experience during a recent conference when someone who was praying for her revealed a whole string of personal facts about her background, all of which were known only to her immediate family and a few to me. This is the word of knowledge in action. It penetrates deeply and uncovers vital information for further ministry. It never provides us with the opportunity of becoming some sort of spiritual voyeur into one another's lives. Like all the gifts it is simply a practical tool to bring an individual and God together.

Faith

Obviously every Christian has faith. Ephesians 2:5 tells us we are saved by grace through faith, while Romans 12:3 reminds us that we have each received a measure of faith from God. Yet there are times when we require an increased level of faith. Take for example the story of Abraham and Sarah. In spite of their age, Abraham continued to believe in God and was rewarded (Heb 11:11).

Faith is recognizing the faithful character of God and expecting to see his promises fulfilled in the here and now. Helen Roseveare in her book *Living Sacrifice* speaks of experiencing the peace of God while working as a missionary in the most terrifying circumstances in the Congo. At the appropriate time God met her needs as she continued to place her trust in him. On a more mundane level, recall the provision of the typewriter mentioned on page 41. Although Mike was very concerned about the fast approaching financial deadline, he knew God would act.

Healing

So much has been written on this subject that we do not intend to add another volume. Suffice it to say that healing is one of the gifts of the Spirit given to the church. There are numerous examples in the Scriptures (e.g. Mt 20:29-34), and it is a gift which is of great value within the church today. We have seen a number of people physically healed—and a number who haven't been. We have learned to start with the small ailments and work upwards—save the wheelchairs till you're comfortable dealing with headaches!

While it may seem strange to take a positive stand for healing when we remain childless, some may say unhealed, we can only say that we have prayed for childless couples and they have conceived and produced children, confirming that God is committed to healing in spite of the questions this gift might raise. Questions do not invalidate the gift but rather fuel our prayer and our seeking of God for practical answers.

Miracles

This gift is evident in the Scripture many times. Take the occasion when the sun stood still in the sky while Joshua was victorious against the Amorites (Josh 10:12-14). When Jesus fed the 5,000 we see the miraculous provision of food for many mouths, and a good few leftovers to demonstrate the abundance of God's provision.

Basically a miracle is when natural laws are suspended and God intervenes directly and supernaturally. Our twentieth-century minds, conditioned by rationality and technology, find such a concept extremely difficult to accept, but we must not let our mental barriers hinder God's powerful working. This is why it is so important to appreciate fully the character of God. He is omnipotent and we must allow him to bring us beyond our reasonable doubts to a level of understanding and faith in line with his word. We could do with a few more miracles in the name of Jesus in this land of ours.

Prophecy

This is not simply a *fore*telling but also a *forth*telling. It is declaring the heart of God in a situation. It will never contradict Scripture, so we have a means of measuring prophecy. Since it is given by a human it has a proportion of humanity in it. The one who prophesies is fully in control of the gift and is not compelled to speak out their prophecy—'The gift of proclaiming God's message should be under the speaker's control' (1 Cor 14:32).

We have found that often in a time of worship a prophecy will address a particular issue or an aspect of God's character using language and illustrations from contemporary life. The heart of the prophecy is in line with the tenor of Scripture, yet it is easily accessible because of the nature of the illustrative framework used. Pastoral images are not that appropriate to an inner-city situation. When Katey was teaching in such an area she was responsible for a trip out and on the journey through the countryside one of the children exclaimed, 'Look, there's a sheep!' to which their companion replied, 'No it's not, it's a cow!' Now one of them was sadly wrong. We worship a God intent on being accessible to people, therefore it is no wonder that he expresses his nature and views in ways that a particular group will easily understand and respond to.

In Matthew 16:17-20 Jesus prophesies about Peter's future ministry. Prophecy has this dimension of foretelling, but the genuine nature of a prophetic word is seen in the fruitfulness of its fulfilment. We should not be so taken up with the practice of the gift that we fail to respond and measure the fulfilment of the word prophesied.

Discernment of spirits

We are involved in a spiritual warfare in which the forces of the enemy lock up and ruin individual lives. These people will not discover freedom and fullness unless the hold of Satan is removed. This is evident in Jesus' dealing with Legion who was ultimately left 'in his right mind' and keen to serve God (Lk 8:26-39). In Luke 13:10-13 Jesus meets a woman crippled by a spirit. Discerning the spirit that had bound her for years, Jesus deals with this demonic hold and she is freed at once.

This gift is vital to our counselling ministry, enabling us to be involved in the effective 'tree surgery' we mentioned earlier in this chapter. As with all the gifts this is a tool for strengthening the body of Christ, both in freeing people from the hold of the enemy and also in identifying positive godly characteristics which are worthy of nurture and encouragement. This latter aspect ensures we identify the people God has chosen for the various essential roles and functions within the church.

Tongues

This gift is best described as a love language to be used in worshipping God (1 Cor 14:2). If your marriage is like ours, then no doubt you have developed a number of phrases which mean something to you but would be meaningless to outsiders. This 'love language' may be intimate, humorous and even apparently stupid, but it is a vital part of your communication with each other. Some couples develop affectionate names for their partners, others adopt almost a whole new vocabulary for use behind closed doors.

Tongues is like this, a language reserved for talking to our heavenly Father. Paul spoke in tongues (1 Cor 14:18) and encouraged the Corinthians to maintain the gift (1 Cor 14:39). It is the only gift which can be used for private benefit as well as for the public purpose of encouraging the body when accompanied by interpretation. Tongues can be used to praise God and to pray earnestly when one doesn't know where to begin praying.

As with all the gifts it is not something we are forced to do by God without any control ourselves, for that is not the character of God. Rather, we choose to speak in tongues, as and when we want to.

Interpretation of tongues

This is the interpretation, not translation, of a message given in tongues in public. It may be expressed as a prayer, a poem of praise, or it may bring a direct word from God to his people.

Other gifts are mentioned in Romans 12:6-8. Take time to look them up now and add them to your existing list of gifts of the Holy Spirit.

The Scriptures urge us to take all God's gifts seriously. We are called to strive for love and set our hearts on spiritual gifts, especially the gift of prophecy (1 Cor 14:1); 'to keep alive the gift that God gave us' (2 Tim 1:6), and reminded 'Each one should use whatever gift he has received to serve others, faithfully administering God's grace in its various forms' (1 Pet 4:10).

However, Katey and I have discovered that though we hear, read and learn much about the gifts of the Spirit we are often sadly lacking in personal experience. In fact, we discovered that our prayer times together provided us with a safe and secure environment to get launched into spiritual gifts and get in some practice. But were we right in practising since we were but two from the body, and could we really claim to be building up the body of Christ through our prayer time together? We believed we could.

Firstly, where two or three gather together Jesus has promised he is there. What is church if it's not where the people of God gather in his presence? We are an expression of church when we pray together. Secondly, as we experimented with and experienced the gifts we were able with a measure of confidence to exercise them within the wider context of our local expression of the body of Christ. This in turn encouraged and enabled others to step out and have a go. If this sounds a little bit unspiritual we can assure you it is not. We worship a practical God who has gifted his church. We need to employ the gifts if we are to obey his word and be what we are called to be in the world today.

The story is told of a very successful and effective managing director who had overseen a large company. His retirement approached and his successor was appointed. Being a man of distinction he visited the retiring managing director and asked him to outline the key to his success in not making wrong decisions. Considering his reply for a moment the managing director simply said, 'Experience.' His successor pressed on and asked, 'How do you get experience?' to which the reply came, 'By making wrong decisions.'(!)

If we are to launch out in using the gifts God has given, we need experience. However, we will make mistakes in gaining that experience, mistakes being a significant part of the learning process. However, God doesn't mind the mistakes if we are sincerely trying to serve and honour him and we recommend you make a good proportion of your mistakes with each other rather than inflicting them all on your local church.

Where to start

We believe the best place to start is with the gifts of tongues, interpretation and prophecy. In 1 Corinthians 14:26-40 Paul outlines the basis for orderly worship, and the instructions he gives about tongues and prophecy give us an indication that the use of these gifts lies within the sphere of human initiative. If God were manipulating mouths for every tongue and prophecy he would not require Paul to give specific guidelines such as, 'If someone is going to speak in strange tongues, two or three at the most should speak, one after the other, and someone must explain what is being said' (1 Cor 14:27), or again, 'You may proclaim God's message, one by one, so that everyone will learn and be encouraged. The gift of proclaiming God's message should be under the speaker's control' (1 Cor 14:31-32). The initiative lies with us and we can choose to go for it or not.

We suggest that together you decide to experiment with these three gifts of tongues, interpretation and prophecy. Stop right now and ensure your partner has read this chapter. Then, if you agree, move into 'Action Stations'.

▶ Action stations

Begin by inviting the Holy Spirit to fill each of you and to fill where you are with his presence. After all, he is a vital personality in the proceedings!

Let's begin with tongues. A number of folk experience some difficulty in getting started with this gift, and this is understandable. I spoke in tongues just a couple of days after I was filled with the Spirit. Katey took about a year to get started. Significantly, Katey had had an inkling she could speak in tongues a while before, but would dismiss the sound which came to mind as something non-sensical which she was making up. It was only as she decided to accept it as God's gift, whether it sounded nonsensical or not, that she discovered her word gave way to a language. Many people we meet have started like this—perhaps you and your partner will.

Nobody has to speak in tongues, but everybody can speak in tongues since it is a gift to be eagerly desired and therefore available to all. If you do want to speak in tongues take a moment to pray, thanking God for his gift of tongues and asking him to release you into it—then wait. That sound, phrase or word that comes to mind is the start of your new love language. Speak it aloud. It may sound nonsensical, but then so does Japanese to me. Partners should encourage each other in the new phrase or word the other is expressing. This is the start. Keep up that phrase or word and more will follow. Don't deny the validity of your new tongue or cease to use it. Rather, as with anything new, use it extensively so that you enjoy it and grow comfortable with it.

Take time to speak in tongues together in praise of God. A lot of folk find it easier to start singing in tongues. Encourage one another and persevere. Praise God with your new-found language. It's been given for that purpose. When you meet a situation for which you don't know how to pray, utilize your new-found tongue. You may well find that the words you use vary—you may identify with Wesley's cry, 'O for a thousand tongues to sing.' There are no limits with God.

We can encourage one another in this gift since one partner may well be a little less confident than the other. I would often take the lead and sing and pray loudly while Katey would draw inspiration from this and follow on but a little more quietly, taking time to build up her own confidence in this gift.

If you are going to exercise the gift of tongues, you will need to ask for the complementary gift of interpretation. It may be that one of you will speak out a short message in tongues and the other will then provide the interpretation. Just pause in the presence of the Lord and speak out the words. As one of you is speaking, the other should stay relaxed, focus on Jesus and simply ask for the interpretation. This may come as a vision in your mind, a sense of what God is feeling, or a clear statement. Once you have an inkling, open your mouth and start speaking.

We can assure you that our early experiences of doing this did not bring forth any earth-shattering revelations, but we found it encouraging and exhilarating to have both been bold enough to participate and to receive simple words of blessing from God through each other. The great thing is to press on with what comes to mind— you may only have a half-formed thought, but express it. You may well embellish it somewhat in an attempt to explain it clearly as you see it; this is our humanity rubbing shoulders with God's divinity. Remember that since the gifts involve human collaboration they will carry a measure of us in them.

The more practice we get, the more comfortable and

confident we will become. And the more comfortable and confident, the more relaxed we are and so the more able to draw upon God's resources and present God's word through these gifts.

We would take the opportunity each time we prayed to incorporate our private love language in praise and intercession, and to give messages in tongues and interpret them. In this way we grew and gained experience. When we contributed in a wider gathering there were others older and more experienced to test the gifts we were utilizing and this acted as a practical safeguard as required.

After you have gained some experience in tongues and interpretation, seek God for the gift of prophecy. Prophecy is similar to interpretation in that as you pray or read Scripture or catch sight of some scene or other you discover that you have a mental picture or clear impression of something to say. It may well not be a complete presentation, but the beginning of something. Only as you speak will you get the whole picture. This is a little nerve-wracking to start with. Many of us have prophesied quite unintentionally in our prayers as we have discharged a burden which we have felt very keenly and which has brought a sense of the presence of God and his perspective to our meeting.

We have found that God has used the gift of prophecy to address us about our circumstances on many occasions. On one occasion God indicated that we were not in an ideal situation from his perspective. One of us had a picture of a fine galleon, sails unfurled catching the wind, but on gazing at the hull it could be seen that the ship was entirely beached and not able to sail before the wind and make for its destination. Not very complicated you say—well no. But in the context of the questions we were asking it spoke volumes and gave us the impetus to put decisions into operation which we felt would refloat the galleon and start it sailing again. Obviously one could interpret the picture in multiple ways, but God had spoken clearly on a specific issue and we decided to be obedient.

Some might object that we conjured up both picture and interpretation since they fitted into the general drift of our thinking at that time. However, God does not play games; just as a father desires no evil for his child, our heavenly Father will not allow us to damage ourselves, which major relocation could do. Also, faith in action takes what God gives and runs with it. So long as it does not contradict Scripture and we are open to chatting it through with other Christians then we can act with confidence.

We have always been ready to communicate what we believe God to be saying with other Christians whom we trust, both because they are friends and because they would not hesitate to say if they thought we were wrong. Often we are so concerned about correction that we stagnate while deliberating about whether God has spoken or not. We have discovered that God finds it difficult to direct stagnant people, but he can more easily govern and guide those on the move as he utilizes their natural momentum. God has always desired a mobile people as the history of Israel in the Old Testament reveals. He will contend with and correct our mistakes while ensuring we reach the right destination.

We are confronted with the challenge of stepping out in faith and experimenting, under God's guidance, with these gifts of tongues, interpretation and prophecy. Utilize your prayer time to gain experience. Perhaps you would like to follow a pattern we adopted for a while. Returning to bed each morning with two steaming mugs of tea. I would revive Katey and then in turn we would each give a message in tongues and an interpretation and then reverse the roles. A very edifying way to start the day! Always remember to retain the ability to laugh and all will be well.

7
Developing a Prayer Life

When we began to experiment with the gifts of the Spirit we discovered a new level of vulnerability. While our marriages do provide a safe and secure environment to gain experience in the gifts of the Spirit, it is amazing just how uncertain one can feel in front of one's partner. This was true for us—we discovered that I felt more threatened than Katey. This boiled down to the fact that as I carefully think everything through, calculating all the options before taking a step forward, I had all my insecurities exposed when I was expected to act on impulse without first checking every final detail out. Katey, however, took to it like a duck to water, being of a more impetuous nature. To this day Katey finds it easier to move in spiritual gifts than me.

However, the vulnerability we experience together is a very positive part of our praying together. Jesus, having died, risen and ascended, promises us three encouragements for our life of discipleship. As we have seen, he gives us his promised Spirit: 'It is better for you that I go away, because if I do not go, the Helper will not come to you. But if I do go away, then I will send him to you' (Jn

16:7). He has also given us his written word, the Bible, which enables us to comprehend more about God and his purposes. In addition he has given us each other:

> I pray not only for them, but also for those who believe in me because of their message. I pray that they may all be one. Father! May they be in us, just as you are in me and I am in you. May they be one, so that the world will believe that you sent me. I gave them the same glory you gave me, so that they may be one just as you and I are one: I in them and you in me, so that they may be completely one, in order that the world may know that you sent me and that you love them as you love me (Jn 17:20-23).

Jesus' prayer, quoted above, reveals that the world will discern our following of him by the quality of the love we extend to one another. Indeed Jesus said, 'And now I give you a new commandment: love one another. As I have loved you, so you must love one another. If you have love for one another, then everyone will know that you are my disciples' (Jn 13:34-35).

Unfortunately we are a very defensive bunch and the very thought of exposure to others causes us to retreat within the castle of ourself, drop the portcullis and lift the drawbridge. However, God is in the business of building practical working relationships. He has established one such between each of us and himself. And he expects to establish the same between us and the other family members who share this planet with us, or more pertinently, our church life with us. While we haven't time to explore this in its wider context, we do need to appreciate its role in our marriages and its place in our prayer life together.

Once we had 'tied the knot' or 'got spliced' or whatever epithet you prefer to use, it slowly dawned on us that we knew very little about the one to whom we had promised to be faithful until death provided a suitable full stop. Perhaps even more intimidating—we each realized how little our spouse knew about us! This posed a problem—in given situations did one behave according to 'expected norms' or was one able to be oneself? We have already looked at this in detail in the section on three-dimensional marriage in chapter 3. Remind yourselves of the practical implications if you cannot remember the content.

Our marriage should allow us to receive counsel and ministry from our partners. We have already said that marriage can be the context in which we are able to encourage our wives to develop experience and confidence in ministry. One way we can do this is let them practise on us men. It is interesting to note that the passage so often quoted to describe the headship of the husband in marriage is immediately preceded by the verse, 'Submit yourselves to one another because of your reverence for Christ' (Eph 5:21). Neither one party nor the other is invited to lord it over the other; each is called to a submissive attitude towards the other. We should each be receptive to whatever God has for us, through whomever he chooses to communicate.

One person we know who has a number of significant spiritual problems and needs has brought God's clear word to us on more than one occasion, and it has been so accurate and to the point that it has made the hairs stand up on the back of our necks. If we have ears to hear, God will constantly communicate with us.

As we progress in getting closer to God, declaring our affection for him and growing increasingly sensitive to his Spirit, we will experience an increased level of vulnerability before each other. When Katey and I were dating there was a diagram much used to describe the male/female Christian relationship. Basically it was a triangle: God was the top corner and we were the two bottom corners, one each side. The object lesson was that the nearer we grew to God the closer we grew to each other, hence intimacy increased and more masks were removed.

We have known what it is to be in the presence of God in worship and then to discover how utterly unclean we are before him. The route forward was to be totally honest with one another over areas in our lives, brought to mind by the Spirit of God, where we were living a lie or exploiting each other. This can be very threatening but also exceptionally enriching. We have verbalized to one another on more than one occasion that since God knows we're rotten anyway and we are only where we are because of his love and grace, why not acknowledge to one another that we are corrupt and helpless as individuals, because in this way we will neither be shocked nor disappointed with one another. We have found that this really takes the pressure off our relationship and means we can be open and honest with no fear that our honesty will be thrown back in our face and our revealed weaknesses exploited at some future date, damaging both the individual concerned and the relationship. As Gerald Coates so eloquently yet economically expresses, 'God will never become disillusioned with us because he never had any illusions in the first place.' We have no right to become disillusioned with one another as a consequence of opening up to each other.

Weaknesses and strengths

While we are not to condemn one another when weaknesses, areas of sin and character deficiencies emerge, neither are we simply to accept them, learning to live with them and accommodating them within our lifestyle.

It was just such a situation that Jesus encountered

when he entered the land of the Gerasenes. These folk had a problem—a guy called Legion. They had tried every means known to them to control or even put an end to his bizarre behaviour, but to no effect. Indeed this character was becoming so well known that had there been travel agents in those days, I've no doubt they would have included him in their brochures as 'local colour'! Eventually he was allowed to take up residence in the graveyard, and the Gerasenes ordered their lives around this frightful and frightening disturbance. By the time Jesus came on the scene they had become so accustomed to accommodating Legion that no one thought to forewarn Jesus or send him a set of directions which avoided the graveyard. As already mentioned, Jesus, when confronted by the man, discerned the spirits and ordered them out, enabling Legion to regain his senses and become an ardent disciple. When the Gerasenes discovered what had happened they were so shocked and disappointed because their whole pattern of life had been reorganized that they begged Jesus to go rather than inviting him for some refreshment and further opportunity to exercise his ministry among them. Read the story for yourself in Luke 8:28-39.

When we discover something out of order in our own lives we are not to push it to the back of our minds and develop a lifestyle and level of Christian experience and service which accommodates it. We are to go up to Jesus, like Legion, and get it dealt with. As Christians we share in the Spirit of Jesus, so we are able to minister him to one another today. This is a vital part of our marital relationship. The sort of ministry to which we are referring is of the tree surgery variety mentioned in the last chapter in the section on the fruit of the Spirit.

One Christmas we were staying with a family and we were amusing ourselves with the children's toys. Katey is convinced that the only reason I want children is so that I can have an excuse to fill the house with toys for my own pleasure. Be that as it may, we had a great time playing with one vehicle which drove across the floor until it encountered an obstacle, at which point it would turn itself over and set off in another direction until meeting some further obstruction when it simply repeated the process. It did this non-stop until it was turned off or the batteries ran out! As Christians we are often confined within borders beyond which we have never explored. The Gerasenes were unable to handle the situation once Legion was set free. The presence and power of God breaking into their well-adjusted lifestyle was too threatening and they asked Jesus to leave, which, being the gentleman he is, he did.

When we pray together and enter into the presence of God, the borders of our own Christian confinement may well be revealed. Areas of weakness, habitual sin and personal difficulty are highlighted, and we need to learn how to minister to one another lovingly and practically. For many of us the plain fact of having to live life in a real and often hostile world has meant that we have learned how to accommodate our weaknesses in order to get through. However, we are very much aware that our lives are anything but peaceful beneath the surface and daily we contend with controlling that turbulence as best we can. Usually it is within our home life, in our marriages, where that turbulence often gives way to a tremendous storm. This is because we feel the least pressure to maintain the mask there or because we think the consequences of such an explosion will not be as damaging to ourselves as in the office or on the shop-floor.

Don't worry when you discover that you are not naturally self-sufficient. All of us bear the marks of our experience of life to date. This has helped to form the people we are. We know a number of areas where we are vulnerable, and should steer clear! We are conscious of weaknesses and work hard at compensating for them. Each of us is also no more and no less than a redeemed sinner, and although the consequences of sin were fully dealt with by Jesus on the cross, we all take time discovering the full extent of our inheritance in Christ as his brothers and sisters. Not only do we need to discover the full extent of that inheritance, we also need to learn how to appropriate it.

We write this in the first instance for mutual assurance. If when you read the section about 'fruit of the Spirit' in the last chapter and concluded that you need a spot of tree surgery, then you have taken a constructive step. We are all in the same boat, Christians saved by grace moving on together and helping one another on as we follow hard after Jesus. It really is the height of arrogance for anyone to believe they are perfect or beyond the need or range of Jesus' ministry. Their position is akin to the Pharisee who denigrated the tax collector in his prayer (Lk 18:9-14). It is Jesus who designates the Father as the vine-dresser or gardener in John 15 and endorses the activity of the gardener as the way to fruitfulness. Ask each other, 'Do you want to be fruitful for Christ?' If the answer is yes, don't be surprised when you discover certain weaknesses or habits becoming highlighted. The gardener is about his work cutting out dead wood that the plant might flourish.

A number of years ago when disaster movies were in vogue a very exciting one was released, fetchingly entitled *The Towering Inferno*. You may have seen it. When we first saw this film at the cinema, Katey virtually crushed my hand such was the intensity of the drama. The film tells the story of a brand-new skyscraper which suffers an outbreak of fire during the opening evening. All the dignatories are enjoying themselves at the very top of the building but by the time the seriousness of the fire is discovered and the 'fireproof' nature of the building proved false, it is too late to leave the building by normal means. The film goes on to show the rescue attempts and the group dynamics of those trapped as individuals seek to ensure that they survive even if it is at the cost of others in the group.

Another plot is also weaved into the film. This gives the reason for the fire in the first place. An enterprising electrical supplier had provided substandard fittings and wiring, well below the original specification, in order to maximize profits. As a result they could not cope with the power demands placed upon them, overheated, shorted and started the fire.

The reason we tell you all this, apart from saving you the cost of the video hire, is that there is an important spiritual principle enshrined in it. The skyscraper did not burn down because of the demands for power placed upon the electrical system. Rather the conflagration was the direct result of an inherent weakness within the construction itself. All that the demand for power did was to expose an inherent weakness, one which eventually led to the destruction of the whole building.

In a similar fashion if we are prepared to walk with God and are committed to spiritual maturity, the Holy Spirit will begin to expose our weaknesses. We may enter a time of great difficulty and pressure. God may appear absent, and the only thing we can focus on is the hurt, the need or the weakness of which we are aware. So often in those times we blame our circumstances or situation when in fact all that is happening is that the circumstances or situation are highlighting an inherent weakness in our life. The route through this is to allow the gardener, God himself, room to remove the weakness and replace it with his strength. We usually require the help, support and prayer of our partner in this since when we expose our weakness to somebody else, as God has exposed it for our consideration, we are less likely either to fail to deal with it properly or to allow it to return to rule our life. God knew what he was about when he left us to one another for our mutual godly benefit. In times of exposure like these we have found that we gain a greater experiential knowledge of the nature of God's inheritance released to us through the death and resurrection of Jesus.

While at Oxford University and attending one of the weekly OICCU Bible readings, we heard a superb exegesis of John 15 given by Ian Barclay. Little did I expect to be working alongside him one day at the Evangelical Alliance. In the Bible study he explained the nature of pruning from a gardener's perspective to help give meaning to the words of Jesus. To this day we remember that the younger the plant and the more vigorously you prune it the more fruitful it will be. A few years later we had a practical demonstration of this when a friend came to tidy up our garden. We had a straggly climbing rose which wandered all over the place. We set off for work that morning leaving our rose in the capable green-fingered hands of our friend. To our shock, on returning home all that was visible was an ugly little stump. To be honest we thought the poor thing was all but dead. We needn't have worried for that summer it flourished and was covered with the most beautiful, pink, scented roses. Do you get the point? We certainly did!

Godly gardening

How does this work out practically in our praying together? We soon discovered that God was more than ready to expose weaknesses in our lives. We then had to decide could we and would we risk levelling with each other and being honest. Fear of rejection and feeling somehow inferior to our partner proved a major obstacle to overcome, but overcome it we did. There was then the question of being able to accept the counsel as well as the prayer of our partner. Prayer is okay maybe, but when we start being corrected and told to repent of certain attitudes by our partner—that's a bit heavy!

All the fundamental lessons previously outlined come into play here. The need to exercise wisdom was paramount in how we broached a subject or an apparent solution, and enabling us to listen without moving onto the defensive or over-reacting. We found that we would often respond by saying, 'I accept that, *but . . .*' and immediately sidestep the point about which the other had challenged or counselled us. There are no 'buts' if we are in a safe and secure environment with someone whom we love and more importantly, in a way, who loves and wants the best for us. We can make mistakes without causing damage; we can learn how to co-operate with God in his gardening activity. It is at this level that the power gifts of the Spirit become very important. Remind yourself of them by turning back to the previous chapter.

One situation in which we discovered something about co-operating with the intelligence God gave us was while selling our house in Leeds. As we prayed Katey had a clear picture of three tall chimneys, the sort one sees at brickworks or being brought down by means of controlled explosion to give a feature for the news! She mentioned this to me and I could see the same in my mind's eye. We prayed on and saw two chimneys come crashing down to the ground. The third remained—a few bricks out from around the base, but not shifting. We asked God to tell us more about the meaning of the picture as we went about our various tasks that week. When we prayed again later in the week we had both recognized the chimneys as obstructions to the sale of our house and the one remaining was symbolic of a materialistic attitude—we wanted to grasp as much from the sale as possible. We repented of the attitude and saw the chimney fall. We celebrated the sale of our house, which had been on the market for several weeks, at that point.

I talked through all that God had shown us with Christian friends. They did not believe that we should drop the price, rather they advised us that selling below market value would be bad stewardship. However, they felt we should be prepared to utilize the proceeds from the sale—all or part—as God directed. We followed this advice and within the week the house sold to someone who had grown up in the road and wanted to get back into it, and we experienced a very loose attachment to the financial proceeds and were able to follow God's instructions cheerfully! The reason for this piece of testimony is to provide an indication of the way God can communicate with us.

When we got involved in 'godly gardening' we discovered God would speak in the same way and we would need to interrupt our prayer times and present, with a measure of grace and diffidence, what we felt God was saying to each other. One incident again concerned the whole area of money. My attitude was one of caution and care. This was healthy up to a point, but did mean that I never had any expectation that there would ever be sufficient finance and lived with a constant tighten-the-belt mentality, always frowning upon, if not forbidding, 'frivolous' extravagances such as a meal out together. Katey identified this one prayer time, receiving a picture of an old, pirate's chest, the lid securely down and sealed. When she had boldly explained this to me she went on to suggest I needed prayer for my lack of expectation and trust in the trustworthiness of God as a provider. This had other implications apart from material ones, Katey was able to minister to me, helping me lay aside my weakness in not trusting God and replace it with a new-found confidence in his practical faithfulness. As if to confirm the reality of the ministry we both had a picture of the lid of the treasure chest open a fraction and the contents beginning to tumble out.

This incident gives some indication of how God can use us to minister to one another, and the way the garden is kept orderly and brought on towards maturity.

We have enjoyed the benefits of ministry to one another in areas of negative attitudes, anger, bitterness and resentment, to name but a few. We have encouraged each other in our service of God and in the particular ways he wants to use us. We have also discovered how to pray for healing for each other with positive results. All this is tremendous fun, and besides being a blessing to us as couples helps us to become a richer resource to the wider body of Christ of which we are a part. As with every area of growing in God, we will have to be prepared to make mistakes and to be wrong. But we will learn through our mistakes. Indeed, as couples we can constructively discuss areas of error or those situations where words don't appear to match up with an individual's experience.

This is the only way we know of becoming familiar with co-operating with God in his gardening duties. It draws us very much closer together and brings a deeper level of security to the relationship. Honesty and openness brings liberty to us as individuals, and when we entrust our weaknesses into the hands of our partners, we make them fiercely loyal and actively committed to our spiritual, physical and emotional welfare.

►Action stations

For all that we have been writing about to become operative, you will need to sit down together to talk around and answer a number of questions. As we continually stress, do ensure you are relaxed and comfortable. Relationships, natural and supernatural, function best when we are in a state of normality.

Together read then think about each of the following questions in turn. Discuss your individual thoughts together after each question before proceeding to the next one.

(1) Am I ready to let God show me who I am and what I'm really like?

(2) Am I ready to let God show me who he is and what he requires?

(3) Am I prepared to stop accommodating areas of my life which are in need of gardening?

(4) Am I prepared to allow the present parameters of my spiritual life to be extended?

After you have discussed your replies together, asked each other questions and generally made some decisions, individually identify any areas in your life—physical, emotional or spiritual—which require a bit of gardening. Do both be honest and practical; if your partner produces sixty foolscap pages of how terrible they are, the basic problem is probably a massive dose of rejection!

Having done this, share your lists with each other and in turn pray, giving permission and actively inviting both God and your partner to be involved in gardening in your life. From now on expect God to speak and act on what he says together.

8

Spiritual Warfare

The book of Daniel in the Old Testament is the story of a man who knew God, could act as his spokesman within his contemporary world and a hostile environment and practised an effective prayer life. In this chapter I want us to consider Daniel's prayer life, not so that we can all copy his pattern of prayer (we should discover what works for us personally in prayer and not just adopt another person's practice) but to draw out some important principles.

Living in Babylon as one of the thousands of Jews exiled there, Daniel was successful at achieving high office in the king's court through diligence and winsomeness, and in no way did he compromise his faith in God (eg. Dan 1:8-16). (Today we need to see increasing numbers of Christian men and women achieving high office in various walks of life and while not compromising their Christian belief, gaining a positive position to influence contemporary society.)

Daniel was obviously a man who loved God and exercised a regular and meaningful prayer walk with him. In chapter 6, verse 10, we discover that even in the face of government legislation banning prayer, except requests made to the king himself for a period of thirty days, Daniel continued his practice of praying to God three times a day, 'just as he had always done'. This led to his encounter with the lions and the king's encounter with the living God.

Daniel was so used to communicating with God and was thus so familiar with his ways that he was greatly used by God in demonstrating his character—for example, interpreting dreams and deciphering writing on the wall. Basically, he practised much that we have been discovering in our prayer life together in this book. However, Daniel, for all his intimacy with God, still ran into a problem that we will meet too. So let's look at it now.

Turn to Daniel 10:12-14. Here we read how Daniel, having fasted and prayed for revelation for three weeks, finally received the answer to his prayers. He is reassured that his request was heard and answered the moment he first prayed, but that his reception of the answer had been held up because of the spiritual conflict that rages between God with his angelic forces on the one hand and the devil with his demonic host on the other.

We need to appreciate that God's character is always to hear and answer our prayers, but sometimes perseverance is demanded for we are all participants in a cosmic struggle which, while not visible to the naked eye, surrounds us on every side. Jesus himself told his disciples, 'Always pray and never become discouraged' (Lk 18:1). Unfortunately a number of us have not, or maybe will not, develop the stamina required to see God's positive answers released to us in the here and now.

A real war

We noticed in an earlier chapter how the prayerful activities of Moses, Aaron and Hur enabled Joshua to overcome the Amalekites. This was because while Joshua fought within the physical realm, Moses and his party mirrored the conflict but in the spiritual realm. Obviously the devil and his crew were not at all keen for Joshua and Israel to succeed. They were, after all, the vanguard of God's good news and demonstrated within their day and generation to all the nations round about that there was one God worthy of worship and his name was Yahweh.

Although we live in a four-dimensional world, often we never perceive beyond dimension three. This fourth dimension was brought home to us very clearly when we were still an engaged couple. It was summer in Oxford and final exams loomed. Katey was preparing for probably her hardest B.Ed. paper when she developed a chronic migraine the afternoon before the exam. When I arrived that evening she told me of the dilemma she was in. If she took the prescribed medicine she would be virtually knocked out for two days, so she would have to tackle the exam in a state of intoxication. However, if she skipped the tablets then the pain with which she would have to contend, not to mention feelings of nausea and spots before the eyes, was just as likely to cause her to perform very badly in the exam. 'What do I do?' she appealed to me.

Feeling very spiritual at that moment, I suggested we go to God for some guidance. We invited a good friend and just went to God in prayer, saying, 'Help!' As we prayed I found myself thinking about the words in James 5:14-15 about healing, particularly about being anointed with oil: 'Is there anyone who is ill? He should send for the church elders, who will pray for him and rub olive-oil on him in the name of the Lord. This prayer made in faith will heal the sick person; the Lord will restore him to health, and the sins he has committed will be forgiven.' We had nothing except Castrol GTX which I did not feel was very appropriate! Instead I leaped up, got an eggcup, filled it with water and prayed something like, 'Lord, we have no oil but you turned water into wine so I guess you can turn this water into oil. Please do so.' We put some of the water—or was it oil?—on Katey's forehead and I prayed. To my surprise I found myself in the middle of a prayer telling the devil to leave her alone. As I prayed Katey suddenly sprang up and shouted, 'It's gone! It's gone!' We all hugged each other and thanked God and Katey was able to take her exam without the slightest trace of a headache.

We realized, as we talked this incident through, that we had stumbled on the fact that there is a fourth dimension to life. We were called by God to be part of an army. We were at war, not at ease, and it is easy to get duped by the enemy into the heresy of plodding through life awaiting our slice of eternal pie in the sky when we die, or to stoically carry our cross through life, maintaining that this is our lot and we must dutifully see it through to the bitter end. God showed us we were engaged in a real war and that we must fight effectively and continually.

A real enemy

The name 'Satan' actually means 'accuser'. It is one of the names given to the devil by the Hebrew writers of Scripture. To the Jews a name is more than a means of identification, it describes the nature of the bearer of the name. Hence God renames Abram 'Abraham' meaning 'father of a multitude', which certainly describes Abraham's unique place in the purposes of God. It is enlightening to work through the Bible looking at names given to the enemy of God, for in doing so you will discover something of his character and therefore the type of traps he lays and attacks he makes on Christians.

The meaning of the name 'Satan' reveals that the enemy is intent on slandering and accusing God's people regardless of whether they are guilty of the accusation. Many folk we have spoken to express a concern that they feel condemned. When asked why they feel condemned, have they said or done anything they should not have done, they are unable to give a clear answer. So long as they are being honest this suggests that they are being toyed with by Satan—being falsely accused but not of anything in particular. When God corrects us he convicts by his Spirit and his conviction is always specific. Just as when the police bring specific charges against someone when they convict him of an offence, so God will identify the specific issue he wants to deal with; he does not leave us wondering what we should do. Satan knows that if he accuses us and we feel condemned we become totally ineffective for God, which is just what he wants.

Satan may be powerful and devious, but he is in no way an equal though opposite force to God. Films like *Star Wars* have given prominence to a spiritual concept which is gaining increasing credence today. This concept sees the universe as a battleground between two equal and opposite forces. However, this idea is not rooted in Christianity, but is an expression of much Eastern religious thought. Another name for Satan in the Bible is 'Lucifer' meaning 'light-bearer' or 'angel of light', for the enemy of God is no more than a fallen angel. He was one of the three archangels with Michael and Gabriel, but he chose to rebel against God, seeking to be like God (Is 14:12-15).

With his angelic host he mounted an armed revolt but was defeated by Michael (Rev 12:7-9) and was literally thrown out of heaven together with his angelic host who had followed his rebellion. It is this angelic host who now serve him in his work of destruction and death throughout the earth, continuing their acts of terrorism against the righteousness and justice of God whom they hate. In Luke 10:18 Jesus refers to the defeat of Satan in the heavens and his expulsion—'I saw Satan fall like lightning from heaven.' He proceeds to encourage his disciples, among whom we may count ourselves, 'I have given you authority so that you can trample on snakes and scorpions and overcome all the power of the Enemy, and nothing will hurt you' (Lk 10:19).

Satan is a created being, for God declares, 'I am the Lord; there is no other god' (Is 45:5). Satan constantly seeks to convince the world of two things, first that he does not exist, secondly that he is the equal and opposite power to God. However, he is ultimately subject to God's authority. We see this in the book of Job where in the very first chapter we encounter Satan in the presence of God. God points out the quality of Job's faithfulness to which Satan responds by maintaining that Job is only faithful because life is good for him. God then gives Satan permission to bring trouble to Job and his family in order to put Job's faithfulness to the test—but note that Satan could only interfere with God's authority and then only to the degree God permitted. Clearly, God rules over Satan.

A real victory

Furthermore, when Jesus died on the cross he dealt the final blow of defeat to Satan. Until that time Satan, with his great weapon of death, held sway over mankind because of the legal authority granted him through the sin of Adam and Eve. But Jesus, totally man and totally

God at one and the same time, burst into human history to engage in personal combat with Satan.

Satan hurled every temptation at Jesus but he resisted all of them. Eventually by ingenious cunning Satan brought Jesus to death on the cross. No doubt he rubbed his hands together gleefully, believing that once Jesus died he would have him totally in his hands, death being the weapon which he wielded over mankind. However, Jesus, although tempted in every way as we are, did not sin and hence Satan could not claim him. Jesus had kept his allegiance to Father God. As he wrestled on that cross with sin, for the first and only time in all eternity cut off from his relationship with his Father, Jesus was recovering what Adam had lost, the opportunity for personal friendship with God. Eventually he proclaimed those great words of triumph, 'It is finished' (Jn 19:30), referring not to his life but his commission, and then chose to release his spirit back to his Father and died. No one took his life, he gave it up entirely of his own will.

Although Satan and his demonic host must initially have been thrilled at this, three days later, as Jesus broke the hold of death and rose from the dead, a wave of concern passed through the hallways of hell. This turned to panic with Pentecost, the proclamation of the gospel and the rapid conversion of the population and the growth of the church. Since then, Satan has been running scared because God has been rescuing men and women from the ranks of Satan and recruiting them in his own invincible army to do battle in spiritual warfare.

The totality of Christ's victory is declared in Colossians 2:13-15—'On that cross Christ freed himself from the power of the spiritual rulers and authorities; he made a public spectacle of them by leading them as captives in his victory procession.' The picture is one of a Roman general returning from a successful campaign and being granted a military parade through the streets of Rome. He would ride at the head of the procession in his chariot, holding one end of a chain draped casually over his shoulder. Following along the line of the chain one would see the defeated generals in neck-irons attached to the chain, shuffling along in the wake of the chariot. Their defeat and subjugation was complete. They were completely in the hands of the victorious Roman general. In the same way Satan and all his forces are completely in the hands of Jesus.

This brings us to our final point about Satan—he is a personality. He thinks, reasons and employs logic—just look at the way he approached Eve. Because of this he will not lay down his arms and recognize his defeat but rather contests every foot of the ground, constantly seeking to convince people that God is not knowable, not good and not available.

To help explain this point I will use the well-known illustration of D-Day and VE-Day. In 1944 the Allies invaded Europe; the occasion is known as D-Day (Decisive Day). From this point on it was evident that the enemy was defeated, but the fighting didn't stop. The Allies had to fight their way through Europe all the way to Berlin before VE-Day (Victory in Europe Day) was celebrated. So with Satan. He has lost the war but continues to fight a rearguard action. Ultimately God will step in and put an end to his activities and there will be no more battles to fight.

We are on the winning side but can expect to be caught up in battles. Satan is committed to robbing men and women of friendship with God, to neutralizing the church in her effectiveness and to interfering adversely in the lives of Jesus' disciples. The Bible describes him as a prowling lion stalking around looking for someone to maul. We should be on our guard against him, but confident because we are on the winning side and 'the weapons we use in our fight are not the world's weapons, but God's powerful weapons which we use to destroy strongholds' (2 Cor 10:4). We are called to conflict; it is part of our commission. We are in a real war, facing a real enemy but enjoying a real victory!

Prayer and warfare

Since the vitality of our relationship with Father God depends to a large degree on prayer, it is obviously an area where we come under intense pressure from the enemy. Prayer is also the means whereby we make ourselves available to co-operating with God in his purpose of ensuring that his kingdom comes and his will is done on earth as it is in heaven. Hence Satan's resistance to such activity.

We mentioned earlier that some answers to prayer are delayed in coming. This is because we are engaged in a cosmic conflict, the full implications of which we will never understand. As Daniel persevered in prayer—and it was a costly experience—so must we. When we wait for answers that apparently elude us, the voice of the enemy rings clearly in our ears using the same words with which he approached Eve: 'Did God really tell you?' (Gen 3:1). He seeks to create doubt, stir up dismay and cause us to lose heart in the reliability of the character of God.

As many will know, we have a major outstanding answer to prayer. For a number of years we have prayed for children, and to some people's surprise we still expect God to answer. We cannot believe that God has altered his revelation since committing it to paper, as it were, in the Bible where we read that he intends man and woman to be fruitful. If we are to accept our childlessness we will have to break with a conviction in the trustworthy nature of the character of God, and that we cannot do. We are also aware that we share a problem, or as Doug Barnett creatively puts it, 'an opportunity for blessing', which was not uncommon to the great men and women of God spoken of in Scripture. And God rewarded their faithfulness—eventually. Indeed, some laugh when I declare that I will go to my grave still believing that we will have children because God is faithful and true to his word.

However, Satan has been very active in bringing pressure on us in this area. Indeed when we first discovered the situation we were in emotional turmoil and found it very hard to take. Fortunately our marital relationship was such that we could include God in the various moods and verbal exchanges that took place; he was even at the receiving end of some of these. As we began to settle down and gained a little perspective, we very simply agreed to place our hand in the hand of God and allow him to bring our lives into line with his word.

The most immediate consequence was that he revealed to us that we were in a very advantageous position. So committed were we to having children, and so much more convinced in his ability than that of the medical establishment, that he had our undivided attention. Never were ears so highly sensitized to the voice of his Spirit; never were lives more ready to be obedient. We also discovered that God immediately removed our focus from children and redirected it onto ourselves. We discovered we were harbouring resentments towards God and people which provided footholds for the enemy.

Prior to becoming Christians we had been involved in ouija and other occult activities, and also had connections with freemasonry and spiritualism. We repented of these activities, loosing their influence through prayer in the name of Jesus, enabling us to enjoy more fully our rich inheritance given by Jesus at the cross. We have learned to actively wield the weapons of our warfare, putting paid to Satan's attempts to influence our lives.

God also showed us how strongly tempted we were to passively acquiesce to childlessness. Such passivity meant that far less energy need be expended, and we could utilize our childlessness constructively within our married life. But passivity, we have found, is food for the devil. It is the start of simply accepting where one is at and not bothering to push on to maturity. Our names might remain written in the Lamb's Book of Life, but we will not take any new ground from the enemy. No, we need to wage warfare actively and with energy.

Other consequences of warfare, we have found, are wounds, exhaustion and a sense of being overwhelmed. We had to dig deep to find the reserves to continue the fight. Often we are intellectually convinced about spiritual warfare, but when we hit the frontline battle we fall down instantly as if someone has slipped the carpet out from under our feet. The reality of spiritual warfare is that it invades every area of our lives and lifestyle. It costs us and we have to decide daily if we will pay the price. We need to urge one another on—Katey and I are always doing this—and develop the camaraderie of an army at war; an army that has won the war but must still complete the final mopping-up operations.

Don't be caught out when a bomb explodes and scatters shrapnel everywhere. Be aware that we are all on active service. Agree together to wage warfare, to persevere to the end and not to fall prisoner to the lies of the enemy.

►*Action stations*

God has fully equipped us for spiritual warfare. Turn to Ephesians 6:10-12. Read this together and take time to discuss what the passage is saying to you as a couple.

Consider in a practical way where you need to engage in active spiritual warfare. Invite God to bring to mind possible chinks in your armour and ask your partner to pray for you in these areas.

9
Meditation

The great Christian apologist C. S. Lewis was first motivated to write stories through an experience he had on a train journey. Standing on the station he picked up a George McDonald book. As he read this he described the experience as one in which his imagination was 'baptized'. That part of his mind which had been dulled over the years was revitalized and to what a great effect when we consider the books he produced such as the Narnia Chronicles. Incidentally, one of the great ways of sustaining the social dimension of your marriage is to read to one another; if you're a family, read together as a family. We do this, more especially over the winter months, reading a chapter aloud together and enjoying the story. We are especially keen on children's literature, and there is a wealth of material available. This can be most creative and we recommend it for strengthening the family bonds.

Ever since I can remember I have had a problem as a Christian with prayer and Bible reading. We've already said that prayer is a problem, but it should not stay like that. It needs to become a delight and an integral part of our lives. I often felt condemned by books or sermons stressing the importance of daily Bible reading and prayer but I did little about it. I would resolve to read at least ten chapters a day to make up for lost time but would soon 'fall by the wayside'.

This all changed radically when I was introduced to Bible meditation. In these days meditation has almost become a 'dirty word' to Christians. This is mainly because of connotations with Eastern religions which place a strong emphasis on meditation. I had a vivid picture of 'Eastern types' involved in many hours of concentrated naval-gazing which I thought odd and very boring! Christians certainly shouldn't meditate by 'emptying' their minds because the mind is soon filled by the enemy, but we can benefit individually and together as couples by meditating on the word of God and thus filling the mind with thoughts about the character and nature of God.

I looked up 'meditation' in an Oxford dictionary and found the following definition: 'To consider thoughtfully, to purpose, to think on, to revolve in the mind.' When talking on meditation I have often explained it by comparing it to eating and enjoying a good meal. There are always parts of a good meal which are exquisite and deserve to be savoured slowly so that they can be enjoyed to the full. I believe that Scripture contains similar 'tasty morsels' which should be chewed over slowly so that the full meaning fills our minds and can be 'digested' into our lives.

When I was introduced to the art of meditation it really did revolutionize my spiritual life. It was something I could do at any time, and for as long or as little as I liked, without having to set a special time aside. When I realized that I was thinking about the word of God for quite a lot of the time, the guilt feelings I had felt for so long left me. I was thinking on God, Jesus and Scripture far more than I had ever done before, even when I had managed to have a 'formal' quiet time.

I began to notice that meditation was actually affecting my life (this is surely what our times with God should do!). Scriptures which I had been meditating upon would come into my mind at times of delight, stress, boredom and frustration and proved a great encouragement to me. It follows that what you spend most time doing eventually dominates your life. I think this is especially true today of television. It is so easy to get caught up in what we see emanating from the box in the corner and to almost live our lives through the eyes of television characters. This is often a result of boredom, when we have little to occupy our time with. If we are not careful boredom can get out of hand and rob us of meaningful relationships because we begin to fill our lives with anything which is a time filler. Marriage can certainly suffer if one or both partners is seeking just to 'fill time'.

I am not at the stage where I can say that my life is totally centred on Jesus but it is affected by Jesus much more than it was, and meditation has greatly helped in this. Let's take a look at some scriptures which talk about meditation.

> Be sure that the book of the Law is always read in your worship. Study it day and night, and make sure that you obey everything written in it (Josh 1:8).
> They find joy in obeying the Law of the Lord, and they study it day and night (Ps 1:2).
> As I lie in bed, I remember you; all night long I think of you (Ps 63:6).
> I will think about all that you have done; I will meditate on all your mighty acts (Ps 77:12).

Psalm 119 has a wealth of references to meditation. Look especially at verses 15, 23, 48, 78 and 148.

Meditation can be used as part of our worship, individually or together with our partner. If you have never meditated before, try the following exercise. Take the opening verse of Psalm 23: 'The Lord is my Shepherd; I have everything I need.' Now start chewing it over, letting your mind wander around it. You may find it easier to do this out loud the first time you try it. There are no right or wrong answers in meditation. God will use times of meditation to speak to us, inspire us and guide us. As I have meditated on that verse in the past, my thoughts have turned to lordship, what it means and what my response should be. I have also found the whole concept of shepherd very rich in meditative terms. I have found it useful to think around the practical things a shepherd does, such as looking after the sheep, tending the injured and knowing each one individually by name, just as Jesus knows us.

Katey has found it useful to place texts around the place so that she notices them at various times. As a housewife she found she spent a lot of time in the kitchen, especially at the sink, so she would place a text behind the taps which she could think on for a few minutes while washing up or peeling the potatoes. She has found that she never 'uses up' a verse and that there is always more to be gleaned in meditation, but she does change the verses regularly. Another good place to stick a verse is above a light switch. You just glance at it and it then plants a seed in your mind which develops during the day.

Meditation requires a 'sanctified imagination'. By that I mean an imagination which God has got hold of and can use to his glory. We all know of situations where our minds have 'run riot' and not always too profitably. God can take such situations and use them to his glory and to our benefit. When Katey started to meditate she found that her mind would often wander off onto what she considered more pressing matters such as the shopping list and what to cook for dinner tonight. It was a real problem until she asked God to sanctify her mind and especially her imagination. Her mind still sometimes wanders off but Scripture exhorts us to 'take every thought captive and make it obey Christ' (2 Cor 10:5). This is only possible by submitting to God and resisting the devil (Jas 4:7).

Meditating as couples can add variety to your prayer life together. It is good for both of you to be actively involved and to have something positive to contribute and bless one another with.

▶ Action stations

Together you are going to meditate on the Lord's prayer. First let's break it up into sections:

(1) Our Father
(2) in heaven:
(3) May your holy name be honoured;
(4) may your Kingdom come; may your will be done on earth as it is in heaven.
(5) Give us today the food we need.
(6) Forgive us the wrongs we have done, as we forgive the wrongs others have done to us.
(7) Do not bring us to hard testing,
(8) but keep us safe from the Evil One.
(9) For yours is the Kingdom and the power and the glory, for ever. Amen.

Here we have nine excellent meditations. If you wanted you could make these the major feature of your prayer life for the next nine days. If it is easiest for you to pray together at the weekends, work your way through the phrases over the next nine weeks.

Following the instructions already given, let the phrases sink into your minds. After about ten minutes, talk through what you have gleaned from considering the phrase. For example, when meditating on 'Our Father' we have found it refreshing to consider how good it is to have a God who is a dad to us. Dads take time with their children; play with them; bring them surprises; cuddle them so that they feel all wrapped up in love and very secure. Our God is just like that.

We discovered that each of us would gain a different perspective with which we were able to enrich our partner's knowledge of God. It also helped us to discover blind spots in our Christian experience—for example, not having any real experience of God as Daddy! We could then invite our partner to pray for us, and could begin a Bible search on the word 'Father' in order to build up a clear picture of the fatherhood of God. Many of us, if we are honest, are not too sure how to read the Bible—and discovering blind spots gives us a purpose for going to the Bible.

Once you've completed meditations on the Lord's prayer, why not start on Proverbs or Psalms? There is a real feast to be had there. Meditating on the Song of Songs will reveal the reality, depth and intimacy of God's love for us.

We have also found that there are many non-biblical sources which can stimulate our imaginations and be a means of directing our thoughts towards God. Take for example the following passage from C. S. Lewis's children's book, *The Lion, the Witch and the Wardrobe* and see how it can become a tool to serve us in our insights into God's work and his world.

He led them up the steep slope out of the river valley and then slightly to the right—apparently by the very same route which they had used that afternoon in coming from the Hill of the Stone Table. On and on he led them, into dark shadows and out into pale moonlight, getting their feet wet with the heavy dew. He looked somehow different from the Aslan they knew. His tail and his head hung low and he walked slowly as if he were very, very tired. Then, when they were crossing a wide open place where there were no shadows for them to hide in, he stopped and looked round. It was no good trying to run away so they came towards him. When they were closer he said,

'Oh, children, children, why are you following me?'

'We couldn't sleep,' said Lucy—and then felt sure that she need say no more and that Aslan knew all they had been thinking.

'Please, may we come with you—wherever you're going?' said Susan.

'Well—' said Aslan, and seemed to be thinking. Then he said, 'I should be glad of company tonight. Yes, you may come, if you will promise to stop when I tell you, and after that leave me to go on alone.'

'Oh, thank you, thank you. And we will,' said the two girls.

Forward they went again and one of the girls walked on each side of the Lion. But how slowly he walked! And his great, royal head drooped so that his nose nearly touched the grass. Presently he stumbled and gave a low moan.

'Aslan! Dear Aslan!' said Lucy, 'what is wrong? Can't you tell us?'

'Are you ill, dear Aslan?' asked Susan.

'No,' said Aslan. 'I am sad and lonely. Lay your hands on my mane so that I can feel you are there and let us walk like that.'

And so the girls did what they would never have dared to do without his permission, but what they had longed to do ever since they first saw him—buried their cold hands in the beautiful sea of fur and stroked it and, so doing, walked with him. And presently they saw that they were going with him up the slope of the hill on which the Stone Table stood. They went up at the side where the trees came furthest up, and when they got to the last tree (it was one that had some bushes about it) Aslan stopped and said,

'Oh, children, children. Here you must stop. And whatever happens, do not let yourselves be seen. Farewell.'

And both the girls cried bitterly (though they hardly knew why) and clung to the Lion and kissed his mane and his nose and his paws and his great, sad eyes. Then he turned from them and walked out on to the top of the hill. And Lucy and Susan, crouching in the bushes, looked after him, and this is what they saw.

A great crowd of people were standing all round the Stone Table and though the moon was shining many of them carried torches which burned with evil-looking red flames and black smoke. But such people! Ogres with monstrous teeth, and wolves, and bull-headed men; spirits of evil trees and poisonous plants; and other creatures whom I won't describe because if I did the grown-ups would probably not let you read this book—Cruels and Hags and Incubuses, Wraiths, Horrors, Efreets, Sprites, Orknies, Wooses, and Ettins. In fact here were all those who were on the Witch's side and whom the Wolf had summoned at her command. And right in the middle, standing by the Table, was the Witch herself.

A howl and a gibber of dismay went up from the creatures when they first saw the great Lion pacing towards them, and for a moment even the Witch seemed to be struck with fear. Then she recovered herself and gave a wild fierce laugh.

'The fool!' she cried. 'The fool has come. Bind him fast.'

Lucy and Susan held their breaths waiting for Aslan's roar and his spring upon his enemies. But it never came. Four Hags, grinning and leering, yet also (at first) hanging back and half afraid of what they had to do, had approached him. 'Bind him, I say!' repeated the White Witch. The Hags made a dart at him and shrieked with triumph when they found that he made no resistance at all. Then others—evil dwarfs and apes—rushed in to help them, and between them they rolled the huge Lion over on his back and tied all his four paws together, shouting and cheering as if they had done something brave, though, had the Lion chosen, one of those paws could have been the death of them all. But he made no noise, even when the enemies, straining and tugging, pulled the cords so tight that they cut into his flesh. Then they began to drag him towards the Stone Table.

'Stop!' said the Witch. 'Let him first be shaved.'

Another roar of mean laughter went up from her followers as an ogre with a pair of shears came forward and squatted down by Aslan's head. Snip-snip-snip went the shears and masses of curling gold began to fall to the ground. Then the orgre stood back and the children, watching from their hiding-place, could see the face of Aslan looking all small and different without its mane. The enemies also saw the difference.

'Why, he's only a great cat after all!' cried one.

'Is *that* what we were afraid of?' said another.

And they surged round Aslan, jeering at him, saying things like 'Puss, Puss! Poor Pussy,' and 'How many mice have you caught today, Cat?' and 'Would you like a saucer of milk, Pussums?'

'Oh, how *can* they?' said Lucy, tears streaming down her cheeks. 'The brutes, the brutes!' for now that the first shock was over the shorn face of Aslan looked to her braver, and more beautiful, and more patient than ever.

'Muzzle him!' said the Witch. And even now, as they worked about his face putting on the muzzle, one bite from his jaws would have cost two or three of them their hands. But he never moved. And this seemed to enrage all that rabble. Everyone was at him now. Those who had been afraid to come near him even after he was bound began to find their courage, and for a few minutes the two girls could not even see him—so thickly was he surrounded by the whole crowd of creatures kicking him, hitting him, spitting on him, jeering at him.

At last the rabble had had enough of this. They began to drag the bound and muzzled Lion to the Stone Table, some pulling and some pushing. He was so huge that even when they got him there it took all their efforts to hoist him on to the surface of it. Then there was more tying and tightening of cords.

'The cowards! The cowards!' sobbed Susan. 'Are they *still* afraid of him, even now?'

When once Aslan had been tied (and tied so that he was really a mass of cords) on the flat stone, a hush fell on the crowd. Four Hags, holding four torches, stood at the corners of the Table. The Witch bared her arms as she had bared them the previous night when it had been Edmund instead of Aslan. Then she began to whet her knife. It looked to the children, when the gleam of the torchlight fell on it, as if the knife were made of stone, not of steel, and it was of a strange and evil shape.

At last she drew near. She stood by Aslan's head. Her face was working and twitching with passion, but his looked up at the sky, still quiet, neither angry nor afraid, but a little sad. Then, just before she gave the blow, she stooped down and said in a quivering voice,

'And now, who has won? Fool, did you think that by all this you would save the human traitor? Now I will kill you instead of him as our pact was and so the Deep Magic will be appeased. But when you are dead what will prevent me from killing him as well? And who will take him out of my hand *then*? Understand that you have given me Narnia for-ever, you have lost your own life and you have not saved his. In that knowledge, despair and die.'

The children did not see the actual moment of the killing. They couldn't bear to look and had covered their eyes.

[Taken from C. S. Lewis, *The Lion, the Witch and the Wardrobe*, Geoffrey Bles 1950, Collins/Fontana Lions 1980, pp 135-41, and used by permission.]

It is, I am sure you will agree, a very moving passage and gives a whole new angle on the crucifixion of Christ. We can have our own spiritual experience expanded by drawing upon the imagination of others in this way. Familiar stories can gain fresh meaning and move us again and often at a deeper level. When Katey and I compared thoughts after this passage we discovered that our eye and mind had been drawn to some of the details of the crucifixion as never before. We were able to have an extended and fruitful period of prayer as a result.

Finally, meditation can help us in our prayers for others. Consider the following poem:

> Lord, how is life for him? Keep a watchful eye,
> Lest that bare cubby-hole apartment drive him to madness.
> Make his pain a dark secret and lend to his face a light
> Meant for two, so the world shall perceive adversity mastered.
> With a lifted cup I salute the force of Your will
> (See the ease of that gesture—my hands held high without trembling.)
> But with Being's radiant armor, protect his soul
> From the jeers of the rabble.
> Unlike him in obscurity, I have a road so plain,
> Polished smooth by the multitudes, memorizing each pebble.
> I can manage this task—just watch me! But please keep him safe.
> From the nooks of insane asylums with spider webbing.
> Do not dispossess him, depriving him of Your strength,
> Do not let Your hand fall carelessly from his shoulder.
> From eternity's alloy of spirit and truth
> Let him fashion a chain and manacles for our sorrow.
> When we stand in Your presence in the next life,
> Asking nothing—except a companionship past all fractures,
> Past the power of angelic trumpets or rending knives,
> We will look at You, ready to give You our answers.

This poem was written by a Russian Christian who until recently was imprisoned for her faith and serving a sentence in a labour camp. By reading her thoughts we will find plenty of fuel for prayer both for her, her husband and others in similar situations. A very fruitful meditation could result from pondering this poem.

Postscript

As you approach the end of this book you are only just beginning an exciting journey of praying together. We hope that the previous chapters have proved both readable and a stimulus to action. However, once you have worked through the book, what then? Will you have the ability to continue to develop an enjoyable prayer life together? Maintaining prayer is always a challenge.

We are convinced that if you continue to put into practice the principles outlined in this book you will establish your own unique and effective life of prayer. Having participated in the 'Action Stations' you have in fact already launched out into praying together. All you need now is to find the time and dive in. As you do this you will establish a personal prayer experience.

Do remember at all times that prayer is for your benefit. So often it exercises a tyranny over us causing us pangs of condemnation. We are not slaves to prayer, rather it is a God-given gift for our welfare. Prayer is our servant, deepening our relationship with our Father and bringing his will and purposes into reality on earth.

It would be unfair to pretend that Katey and I, having

discovered the lessons written about here, have found prayer plain sailing. We have struggled to keep up our practice of prayer. There are even times when we have ceased praying altogether, but at such times we don't beat ourselves or each other with a club of guilt but simply sit down and re-evaluate our situation. The process of overcoming embarrassment with regard to praying together has enabled us to talk the situation through calmly, draw conclusions and take practical decisions to move us forward.

So often we seem to establish a pattern for prayer and no sooner having done so we grow uncomfortable with it or just plain bored. At other times we have to recognize that the framework we have been using has grown stale and so our praying together has become mechanical and lifeless—a duty maintained and little more. One way to combat this is to take the positive steps suggested by us to keep prayer alive, fresh and vibrant.

In one of his books Juan Carlos Ortiz recounts the day he decided the prayer meeting had grown stale. Seated in a room with a group of hallelujah hearties he decided to break the mould once and for all. It was as if the affirmations of 'Thank you Jesus', 'Amen', 'Glory' etc. which regularly punctuated the prayer time were simply tumbling from people's lips through habit. Ortiz took everyone out of the room and into the open air. He then encouraged them to keep their eyes open, move around and praise God for the many glorious evidences of his creation. The expressions of praise were to be clear vocal declarations—and so the fun began. The lesson is not to troop out into the back-garden and do likewise (although you might like to give it a go), rather it is that we need constantly to discover fresh ways of praying that prevent us from stagnation.

We often pray when out walking the dog. As we stroll

along the beach we spontaneously thank God for the many good things around us or for how good it is to be related to God and to each other. Such spontaneity is itself a creative stimulus for each partner and in no time at all a praise meeting has broken out on the beach—well, two of us getting excited and a bemused dog looking on.

When visiting friends some of my most pleasurable moments have been when their children, having looked me over carefully for some time, have all of a sudden crossed the room with arms uplifted in a silent request for a good cuddle, demonstrating that I've been accepted by them. There is something very heartwarming about such spontaneity. I believe we need to find ways of releasing that kind of spontaneity within our worship as churches whether our liturgy be formal or free.

When walking the dog it is not just praise and worship that flows from our lips. We also pray for specific situations as we walk along, breaking into our conversation with an appeal to God about what we have been discussing before resuming our conversation once again. I personally find a walk very helpful in talking through all the things on my mind and Katey proves a most helpful sounding-board. As we express all our concerns and dreams and consider the plight of various individuals and groups it seems only natural to pray there and then. Our prayer is increasingly and effectively woven into the everyday fabric of our lives.

But what if . . .

We have learned over the years that the biggest impediment to action is one small three-letter word—'but'. It seems that for every proposal someone can be relied upon to find an exception. Few will accept this as the exception which proves the rule.

Often the exceptions pinpointed relate to circumstances. We need to recognize that there are some circumstances that we cannot change; however, circumstances always contain the capacity to change us. It is in this area that some of our greatest apparent difficulties may emerge.

(1) But what if we've young children?

Since we cannot speak from experience, we have chatted with couples with young children and noted their wise counsel.

As with all 'what if' questions, there has to be the desire and commitment to look beyond the problem to a solution. Obviously time is at a premium and opportunity to pray very limited. That is where spontaneity is more helpful, and why establishing an effective pattern of prayer from courtship onwards pays dividends. For example, why not chat to God while bathing the baby or feeding the youngster. Recognizing that evenings are rest and recovery periods for Mum, seek to ensure a time of worship over breakfast. If this happens to coincide with the baby's feed-time at 6 a.m., so be it. Or if it entails bringing a tray of tea and toast upstairs to the bedroom, then do it. The arrival of children demands a reordering of lifestyle, including spiritual life. Perhaps Dad could find a short verse at the start of the day for both to meditate on during the day and then talk over the fruit of that meditation as you sit facing each other in the bath at 8 p.m. that night! Just a suggestion.

(2) But what if I'm on shift work?

You could try the meditation principle suggested above and talk it through when you link up. If you are not going to see each other, leave a verse on a postcard ready for your partner along with the other special treats which help keep romance alive. When you both have a day off together, give yourselves time as a couple to go for a walk or out for a drink and talk and pray as you go. Try to ensure you have a word of encouragement or a prophecy for your partner for when you are together. If work means being apart for a long time agree beforehand targets to focus prayer on each day while separated. When I travelled a lot with BYFC Katey and I would agree what part of the Bible we would read, keep to it as best we could and expect to have a feast to enjoy together when reunited.

(3) But what if I give up?

The simple answer is don't. The practical reply is start again, maybe utilize this book once more as a springboard to action. Don't become a slave to your past—shrug it off and have another go. As a Christian you have all the resources you need to overcome hindrances in prayer. Once you recognize that, make the necessary allowances then get started at a level at which you feel comfortable. You will then discover how enjoyable and effective the whole business of prayer is.

We urge you from this point on to begin your own unique journey and establish a personal testimony of praying together with your partner.